THE CREATIVITY CONUNDRUM

ESSAYS IN COGNITIVE PSYCHOLOGY

North American Editor:
Henry L. Roediger, III, Washington University in St. Louis

United Kingdom Editors:
Alan Baddeley, University of Bristol
Vicki Bruce, University of Stirling

Essays in Cognitive Psychology is designed to meet the need for rapid publication of brief volumes in cognitive psychology. Primary topics include perception, movement and action, attention, memory, mental representation, language, and problem solving. Futhermore, the series seeks to define cognitive psychology in its broadest sense, encompassing all topics either informed by, or informing, the study of mental processes. As such, it covers a wide range of subjects including computational approaches to cognition, cognitive neuroscience, social cognition, and cognitive development, as well as areas more traditionally defined as cognitive psychology. Each volume in the series will make a conceptual contribution to the topic by reviewing and synthesizing the existing research literature, by advancing theory in the area, or by some combination of these missions. The principal aim is that authors will provide an overview of their own highly successful research program in an area. It is also expected that volumes will, to some extent, include an assessment of current knowledge and identification of possible future trends in research. Each book will be a self-contained unit supplying the reader with a well-structured review of the work described and evaluated.

Titles in preparation
United States
Brown, *The Deja-Vu Experience*
Gernsbacher, *Suppression and Enhancement in Language Comprehension*
Johnson, *The Psychological and Social Processes of Reality Monitoring*
Robertson, *Space, Objects, Brains, and Minds*
Park, *Cognition and Aging*

United Kingdom
Cornoldi and Vecchi, *Visuo-spatial Representation: An Individual Differences Approach*
Jones and Macken, *Auditory Distraction and Cognition*
Schyns, *Less than Meets the Eyes: Perceiving the World in Categories*
Morton, *Headed Memories*
Scheinberger, *Recognizing Faces*
Coventry and Garrod, *Seeing, Saying, and Acting*

WITHDRAWN

THE CREATIVITY CONUNDRUM:

A Propulsion Model of Kinds of Creative Contributions

Robert J. Sternberg
Yale University

James C. Kaufman
Educational Testing Service

Jean E. Pretz
Yale University

Psychology Press
New York • London • Brighton

Published in 2002 by
Psychology Press
29 West 35th Street
New York, NY 10001

Published in Great Britain by
Psychology Press Ltd
27 Church Road
Hove, East Sussex
BN3 2FA

Psychology Press is an imprint of the Taylor & Francis Group.

Library of Congress Cataloging-in-Publication Data
Sternberg, Robert J.
    The creativity conundrum : a propulsion model of kinds of creative contributions / Robert J. Sternberg, James C. Kaufman, Jean E. Pretz
        p. cm. — (Essays in cognitive psychology)
    Includes bibliographical references and indexes.
    ISBN 1-84169-012-0
    1. Creative ability. 2. Creative thinking. I. Kaufman, James C. II. Pretz, Jean E. III. Title. IV. Series.

BF408 .S757 2002
153.3′5—dc21

                                                    2001048477

This book is dedicated by all of us to all those people around the world who, because they live in an atmosphere of political, social, or economic oppression, never have the opportunity to bring to germination the creative seeds of ideas they carry within them.

This book is further dedicated by James Kaufman to Alan S. Kaufman and Nadeen L. Kaufman, with love, respect, and gratitude.

CONTENTS

ABOUT THE AUTHORS

Robert J. Sternberg is IBM Professor of Psychology and Education and Director of the Center for the Psychology of Abilities, Competencies, and Expertise at Yale University. His doctorate in psychology is from Stanford and he has four honorary doctorates. He is the author of more than 850 articles and books on human abilities.

James C. Kaufman is an Associate Research Scientist at the Center for New Constructs at Educational Testing Service. He received his doctorate in psychology from Yale University. He is the author of three other books, published or in press, and is the Associate Editor of *Research in the Schools*.

Jean E. Pretz is a doctoral candidate in the psychology department at Yale University. She received a B.A. in psychology and music from Wittenberg University, Springfield, OH, and an M.S. from Yale University. In 2001, she received the American Psychological Society Student Caucus Student Research Competition Award. Her interests include creativity, intuition, expertise, and transfer in problem solving.

PREFACE

There are tens of thousands of artists, musicians, writers, scientists, and inventors today. What makes some of them stand out from the rest? Why will some of them become distinguished contributors in the annals of their field and others be forgotten? Although many variables may contribute to determining who stands out from the crowd, certainly creativity is one of them. The standouts are often those who are doing particularly creative work in their line of professional pursuit. Are these highly creative individuals simply doing more highly creative work than their less visible counterparts, or does the creativity of their work also diverge in quality?

In this book, we argue that creative contributions differ not only in their amounts but also in the kinds of creativity they represent. For example, both Sigmund Freud and Anna Freud were highly creative psychologists, but the nature of their contributions seems in some way or ways to have been different. Sigmund Freud proposed a radically new theory of human thought and motivation and Anna Freud largely elaborated on and modified Sigmund Freud's theory. How do creative contributions differ in quality and not just in quantity of creativity? This book will address this question.

We further argue in this book that the kind of creativity exhibited in a creator's works can have at least as much of an effect on judgments about that person and his or her work as does the amount of creativity exhibited. In many instances, it may have more of an effect on these judgments.

This book is based on a theory first proposed by Sternberg (1999c) and then elaborated on by Sternberg, Kaufman, and Pretz (2001). It is written for anyone interested in creativity—psychologists, philosophers, cognitive scientists, writers, artists, and laypeople. We believe it will help anyone understand the different forms creative contributions can take.

Preparation of this book was supported by Grant REC-9979843 from the National Science Foundation and by a government grant under the

Javits Act Program (Grant R206R000001) as administered by the Office of Educational Research and Improvement, U.S. Department of Education. Grantees undertaking such projects are encouraged to express freely their professional judgment. This book, therefore, does not necessarily represent the positions or the policies of the U.S. government, and no official endorsement should be inferred.

We are grateful to Cynthia Blankenship for assistance in the preparation of the manuscript. We also thank David K. Hecht, Christopher C. Henrich, Alan S. Kaufman, Nadeen L. Kaufman, Paul B. Murphy, Renate Otterbach, and David A. Pizarro for comments on portions of the manuscript. We thank Henry Roediger, III, for commissioning this manuscript. And we are grateful to two anonymous reviewers for their very helpful comments on the manuscript.

Most of all, we are thankful to the supportive colleagues with whom we have worked and the institutions in which we have worked that have enabled us to give expression to our own creative ideas. We are most keenly aware of the fact that many people would like few things more than to nurture and give expression to their creative ideas, but because of the environments in which they live, never get the chance.

RJS, JCK, JEP

The Propulsion Model of Creative Contributions

☐ Introduction

Creativity is the ability to produce work that is novel (i.e., original, unexpected), high in quality, and appropriate (i.e., useful, meets task constraints) (Lubart, 1994; Ochse, 1990; Sternberg, 1988a, 1999b; Sternberg & Lubart, 1995, 1996). Creativity is a topic of wide scope that is important at both the individual and societal levels for a wide range of tasks. At an individual level, creativity is relevant, for example, when solving problems on the job and in daily life. At a societal level, creativity can lead to inventions, new scientific findings, movements in art, and social programs. The economic importance of creativity is clear because new products or services—such as the Internet—create jobs. Furthermore, to remain competitive, individuals, organizations, and societies must adapt existing resources to changing task demands.

Creativity may be viewed as taking place in the interaction between persons and their environments (Amabile, 1996; Csikszentmihalyi, 1996, 1999; Feldman, 1999; Feldman, Csikszentmihalyi, & Gardner, 1994; Sternberg & Lubart, 1995). Thus the essence of creativity cannot be captured as an intrapersonal variable. We can characterize a person's cognitive processes as more or less creative (Finke, Ward, & Smith, 1992; Rubenson & Runco, 1992; Weisberg, 1986) or the person as having a more or less creative personality (Barron, 1988; Feist, 1999). Further, we can describe the person as having a motivational pattern that is more or less typical of creative individuals (Hennessey & Amabile, 1988), or even as having background variables that more or less dispose that person to think creatively (Simonton, 1984, 1994). But we cannot fully judge that person's creativity independent of the context in which the person works.

For example, a contemporary artist might have thought processes, personality, motivation, and even background variables similar to those of Monet, but that artist, painting today in the style of Monet, probably would not be judged to be so creative as Monet. Unless the contemporary artist introduced something new, he or she might be viewed as imitative rather than creative.

The importance of context is illustrated by creative discovery versus rediscovery. For example, Langley, Simon, Bradshaw, and Zytgow (1987) developed BACON and related programs to rediscover important scientific theorems that were judged to be creative discoveries in their time. The processes by which these findings are made via computer simulation are presumably not identical to those of the original discoverers. One difference is that contemporary programmers can provide, in their programming of information into computer simulations, representations and particular organizations of data that may not have been available to the original creators. But putting aside the question of whether the processes are the same, a rediscovery might be judged to be creative with respect to the rediscoverer, but would not be judged to be creative with respect to the field at the time the rediscovery is made. Ramanujan, the famous Indian mathematician, made many such rediscoveries. A brilliant thinker, in his early life he did not have access to much recent mathematical literature and so unwittingly regenerated many discoveries of others.

☐ Creativity as a Neglected Research Topic

Sternberg and Lubart (1996) have observed that, historically, creativity has been a neglected research topic in psychology. As early as 1950 J. P. Guilford, in his Presidential Address to the American Psychological Association, challenged psychologists to pay attention to this neglected but extremely important attribute. Guilford reported that fewer than two-tenths of 1% of the entries in *Psychological Abstracts* up to 1950 focused on creativity.

Interest in creativity research began to grow in the 1950s, and a few research institutes concerned with creativity were founded. However, several indicators of work on creativity show that it remained a relatively marginal topic in psychology until recently. Robert Sternberg and Todd Lubart (1996) analyzed the number of creativity references in *Psychological Abstracts* from 1975 to 1994. They searched the computerized PsychLit database of journal articles using the database keywords of "creativity," "divergent thinking," and "creativity measurement." (These terms are assigned by the database to articles whose content concerns primarily the subject of creativity.) They also identified additional entries that contained the word stem "creativ-" somewhere in the title or abstract, but were not indexed by one of the keywords for creativity. They examined a random subset of these additional entries and found that they did not concern creativity to any notable extent, and thus were excluded from studies of creativity. The result of this analysis is that approximately .005 (one-half of 1%) of the articles indexed in *Psychological Abstracts* from 1975 to 1994 concerned creativity. For comparative purposes, articles on reading accounted for approximately 1.5% of the entries in *Psychological Abstracts* during the same 20-year period, three times greater than for creativity.

If we look at introductory psychology textbooks as another index, we find that creativity is barely addressed. Whereas intelligence, for example, comprises a chapter or a major part of one, creativity gets a few paragraphs (e.g., Gleitman, 1986). There are rarely courses on creativity in major psychology departments, although such courses are sometimes offered in educational psychology programs. Part of the problem is that creativity does not fit into any single traditional area of psychology. It crosses clinical, cognitive, differential, personality, developmental, and social psychology, so that each area is likely to see it as fitting into some other.

Sternberg (1999c) has presented what he refers to as a propulsion model of creative contributions. The idea is that creative contributions "propel" a field forward in some way—they are the result of creative leadership on the part of their creators. The propulsion model is a descriptive taxonomy of eight kinds of creative contributions. Although these contributions may differ in the extent of creative contribution they make, there is no a priori way of evaluating *amount* of creativity on the basis of the *kind* of creative contribution. Certain kinds of creative contributions probably tend, on average, to be more novel than are others. But creativity also involves quality of work, and the kind of creative contribution a work makes does not make necessarily predict the quality of that work.

The eight kinds of creative contributions follow.

1. *Replication* shows that a given field is where it should be. The propulsion is intended to keep the field where it is, rather than moving it forward.
2. *Redefinition* redefines where the field currently is. The current status of the field thus is seen from a new point of view.
3. *Forward incrementation* moves the field forward in the direction in which

it already is moving, and the contribution takes the field to a point for which others are ready.

4. *Advance forward incrementation* moves the field forward in the direction it is already going, but the contribution moves beyond where others generally are ready for the field to go.

5. *Redirection* moves the field from where it is toward a new and different direction.

6. *Reconstruction/redirection* directs the field back to where it once was (a reconstruction of the past) so that the field may move onward from that point, but in a direction different from the one it took from that point onward.

7. *Reinitiation* directs the field to a different and as yet not reached starting point and then moves the field in a different direction from that point.

8. *Integration* puts together aspects of two or more past kinds of contributions that were viewed as distinct or even opposed. This kind of contribution shows particularly well the potentially dialectical nature of creative contributions, in that it merges into a new Hegelian type of synthesis two ideas that formerly may have been seen as opposed (Sternberg, 1999a).

The creative contributions described above are kinds of qualitatively distinct (with the possible exception of forward incrementation and advance forward incrementation). However, within each kind, there can be quantitative differences. For example, a forward incrementation may represent a fairly small step forward for a given field, or it may represent a substantial leap. A reinitiation may restart an entire field or just a small area of that field. Moreover, a given contribution may overlap categories. Thus, when we mention in this book various contributions as examples of the various categories, we do not wish to suggest that they uniquely exemplify those categories. The examples we give are from science and technology, arts and letters, and popular culture, but we believe that the model applies to creativity in all fields.

Thus, when people are creative, they can express it in different ways. The means of expression depend upon the model of kinds of creative contributions one accepts. People's ways of being creative may be, in part, a matter of intention, and, in part, an accident. For example, we and our colleagues who have worked at the Center for the Psychology of Abilities, Competencies, and Expertise (PACE Center) at Yale like to ask ourselves, when we generate what we hope are creative ideas, whether these ideas are likely to be distinctive from those of others. We often prefer, if possible, to produce paradigm-breaking or, at least, paradigm-bending ideas. But, other people may prefer to work within existing paradigms. Often, when we come up with an idea we like, we do not think at all about the kind of idea it is. We pursue it merely because we wish to.

It is important to note that whereas there is a large difference between *kind* of creativity and *amount* of creativity, there is probably some correlation. For example, conceptual replications are almost certainly less creative, on average, than are reinitiations. But the correlation will be far from perfect. For example, one forward incrementation may be that next discovery that everyone has been seeking, rendering the contribution highly novel and high in quality, and thus very creative. At the same time, a given reinitiation may be path breaking but useless (such as the proposal that all people on Earth move to Jupiter immediately).

What is creative contribution and why do we need a taxonomy of kinds of creative contributions? A consensual definition of a creative contribution is of something that is (a) relatively original and (b) high in quality vis-à-vis some purpose (see Sternberg & Davidson, 1994; Sternberg & Lubart, 1995, 1996). Starting with creative contributions rather than creative contributors can have several advantages.

First, a given contributor may make a variety of kinds of contributions. The contributor thus is not limited to any one kind of creative contribution described in this book. Contributions may be primarily of a given kind, but creators may not be. For example, much, but certainly not all, of Picasso's work set off in strikingly original and bold directions. Through the proposed theory, one can evaluate individual works of a creator and not just the "average" or typical kind of work the creator produced.

Second, even if contributors usually make a certain kind of contribution, observing differences in the kinds of contributions individuals make can help elucidate differences in the kinds of creativity the contributors typically tend to show.

Third, the emphasis on contributions rather than creators underscores the point that people can modify the kinds of contributions they make. Someone early in his or her career may be afraid to depart too much from accepted ways of doing things, for fear that such a departure will put his or her career at risk. Later, however, especially after establishing a favorable reputation, the creator may be willing to take risks. Even from the days when composers had to compose music or artists to paint works to please their royal patrons, creative individuals have always operated under societal constraints. Given the importance of purpose, creative contributions must always be defined in some context. If the creativity of an individual is always judged in a context, then it will help to understand how the context interacts with how people are judged. In particular, what are the kinds of creative contributions a person can make within a given environment? Most theories of creativity concentrate on attributes of the individual (see Sternberg, 1988a, 1999b). But to the extent that creativity is in the interaction of person with context, we would need as well to concentrate on the individual's work relative to the environmental context.

The most obvious way to distinguish among creative contributions might be in the domains in which they are made, such as art, biology, literature, or music. Csikszentmihalyi (1996; Csikszentmihalyi & Rathunde, 1990) has made a further distinction between the domain and the field. A *domain* is a formal body of knowledge such as in art or biology, whereas a *field* is the social organization of the domain. The field is typically the source of judgments as to whether contributions in a domain are creative. The basis of creativity in the interaction between individual and context is shown by the fact that what a field judges to be creative at one time might differ from what it judges to be creative at another. The works of Bach or Van Gogh are now viewed as more creative by the members of their fields than at the time the works were done. At a given time, the field can never be sure of whose work will withstand the judgments of the field over time (such as that of Mozart) and whose work will not (such as that of Salieri).

A taxonomy of creative contributions needs to ask not just what domain a work belongs in, but also what kind of creative contribution it is. What makes one work in biology more creative or creative in a different way from another work in the same field, or what makes its creative contribution different from that of a work in art? Thus, a taxonomy of domains of work is insufficient to elucidate the nature of creative contributions. A field needs a basis for scaling how creative contributions differ quantitatively and, possibly, qualitatively.

☐ Some Existing Taxonomies of Kinds of Creative Contributions

Tests of creativity (e.g., Torrance, 1974) typically provide scores that assess both quantitative and qualitative aspects of performance (Plucker & Renzulli, 1999). For example, the Torrance tests can be scored for originality of responses (how unusual each response is), flexibility (how varied the responses are), and fluency of responses (how many unusual responses there are). These types of scores also serve as a basis for a taxonomy of aspects of creativity (Guilford, 1975; Michael & Wright, 1989). But the test scores are largely atheoretical.

Theorists of creativity and related topics have recognized that there are different kinds of creative contributions (see reviews in Ochse, 1990; Sternberg, 1988a; Weisberg, 1993). For example, Kuhn (1970) distinguished between normal and revolutionary science. Normal science expands upon or otherwise elaborates upon an already existing paradigm of scientific research, whereas revolutionary science proposes a new paradigm. Revolutionary thinkers have included Newton and Einstein in the field of physics, Darwin and Wallace in biology, Braque and Picasso in the visual arts, and Freud and Wundt in psychology. Darwin's contribution is particularly well analyzed by Gruber (1981). Normal science corresponds to our paradigm-accepting kinds of creativity (i.e., replication, redefinition, forward incrementation, and advance forward incrementation), whereas revolutionary science corresponds to our paradigm-rejecting kinds of creativity (i.e., redirection, reconstruction/redirection, and reinitiation). Integration does not fit comfortably into either of Kuhn's categories, as it is paradigm-synthesizing in character.

Gardner (1993, 1994) also described different types of creative contributions individuals can make. They include (a) the solution of a well-defined problem, (b) the devising of an encompassing theory, (c) the creation of a "frozen work," (d) the performance of a ritualized work, and (e) a "high-stakes" performance. These distinctions do not map well onto our distinctions, we believe, because they seem to refer to vehicles for creative expressions rather than to kinds of creativity.

Other bases for distinguishing among types of creative contributions also exist. For example, psychoeconomic models such as those of Rubenson and Runco (1992) and Sternberg and Lubart (1991, 1995, 1996) can distinguish different types of contributions in terms of the parameters of the models. In the Sternberg–Lubart model, contributions might differ in the extent to which they "defy the crowd" or in the extent to which they redefine how a field perceives a set of problems. Thus, this model deals primarily with the paradigm-rejecting forms of creativity (i.e., redirection, reconstruction/redirection, and reinitiation). Simonton's (1997) model of creativity also proposes parameters of creativity, and contributions might be seen as differing in terms of the extent to which they vary from other contributions and the extent to which they are selected for recognition by a field of endeavor (see also Campbell, 1960; Perkins, 1995; Simonton, 1997). But in no case were these models intended *explicitly* to distinguish among kinds of creative contributions. Rather, the models can be extrapolated to suggest how creators might differ.

A view that is relevant to taxonomies of creativity has been proposed by Gough and Woodworth (1960), who discussed stylistic variations among professional research scientists. The styles include zealots, initiators, diagnosticians, scholars, artificers, estheticians, and methodologists. For example, a zealot proposes a cause and then becomes extremely strongly identified with that cause, sometimes with only minimal empirical support. A methodologist concentrates on and takes great care with the methodology of his or her contributions and perhaps with the innovation inhering in the methodology, possibly at the expense of paying attention to the substantive contribution. These distinctions seem more to be among styles or ways of expressing creativity than among kinds of creativity as specified in the propulsion model.

Maslow (1967) distinguished more generally between two types of creativity, which he referred to as primary and secondary. Primary creativity is the type of creativity a person uses to become self-actualized—to find fulfillment. Secondary creativity is the type of creativity with which scholars in the field are more familiar—the type that leads to creative achievements of the sort typically recognized by a field. The propulsion model seems to apply largely to what Maslow referred to as secondary creativity, rather than to his notion of primary creativity.

Disagreements among scholars in the field of creativity also may reflect different types of creative contributions. Ward, Smith, and Finke (1999) noted three such apparent disagreements and how these may reflect differences in types of creativity rather than in what "truly" underlies creativity. One apparent disagreement is regarding goal-oriented versus exploratory creativity. Ward and his colleagues noted that there is evidence to favor the roles of both focusing (Bowers, Regehr, Balthazard, & Parker, 1990; Kaplan & Simon, 1990) and of exploratory thinking (Bransford & Stein, 1984; Getzels & Csikszentmihalyi, 1976) on creative thinking. It may be, however, that both kinds of thinking can lead to creative work of different types. A second distinction made by Ward and his colleagues is between domain-specific (Clement, 1989; Langley et al., 1987; Perkins, 1981; Weisberg, 1986) and universal (Finke, 1990, 1995; Guilford, 1968; Koestler, 1964) creativity skills. Yet both kinds of skills may be relevant to creativity. They suggested, for example, that efficient exploration of a preinventive structure depends on knowledge and experience, but that general methods may be relevant in designing a new form of transportation. Finally, Ward and his colleagues distinguished between unstructured (Bateson, 1979; Findlay & Lumsden, 1988; Johnson-Laird, 1988), and structured or systematic (Perkins, 1981; Ward, 1994; Weisberg, 1986) creativity. Unstructured creativity suggests that randomness, or perhaps blind variation in the generation of ideas, plays a major role in creativity (see, e.g., Cziko, 1998; Simonton, 1998), whereas structured creativity suggests that some kind of system is highly involved in the generation of ideas (see, e.g., Sternberg, 1998). Again, Ward and his colleagues saw structure and lack of structure as complementary rather than contradictory. Indeed, different biological mechanisms—such as in levels or types of cortical activation—may underlie different kinds of creativity (Martindale, 1999).

In this book, we propose a propulsion model of kinds of creative contributions (see also Sternberg, 1999c). The model differs from many previous models in explicitly being intended to distinguish kinds of creative contributions and in systematically basing the distinctions among these various kinds of contributions on a single unified spatial representation.

☐ The Propulsion Model of Kinds of Creative Contributions

A Spatial Representation for Contributions to a Field

Imagine a multidimensional space of unknown but high dimensionality that represents all work in a given field at a given time. This space most easily might be conceptualized as the space that represents the union of a series of local subspaces (see Sternberg, Tourangeau, & Nigro, 1979; Tourangeau & Sternberg, 1981, 1982). Figure 1.1 shows a segment of what such a series of local subspaces and the space might look like for the contemporary field of psychology.

One local subspace might divide contributions by their subfield of endeavor, as shown in Figure 1.1(a)—social psychology, cognitive psychology, clinical psychology, and so forth. Because any field can be viewed as prototypically defined (Rosch, 1978), a given contribution might be more or less close to the prototype of one or more of these subfields. Thus a study of children's eyewitness testimony would have some loading on the dimension of "cognitive psychology" to represent the extent to which it typifies studies in cognitive psychology; but it also would have a loading on the dimension of "social psychology" because it makes a contribution to that subfield and on the dimension of "developmental psychology" because it makes a contribution to that subfield as well.

A given work also makes a contribution with regard to methodology. A study can vary in the extent to which it makes use of experimental, naturalistic, case-study, and other types of methods, as shown in Figure 1.1(b). Some studies use only one method to the exclusion of all others, in which case they would have a nonzero loading on one dimension and a zero loading on all others in this subspace; other studies use a combination of methods, in which case they would have multiple nonzero loadings. For example, a study of eyewitness testimony in children might use interviews within the context of an experimental design.

A study also can vary in the extent to which performance draws on different types of mental processes, such as perception, memory, emotion, and so forth (each of which of course could be further subdivided), as shown in Figure 1.1(c). For example, the study of children's eyewitness testimony would call upon the perceptions, memories, emotions, reasoning, and other processes of the participants involved.

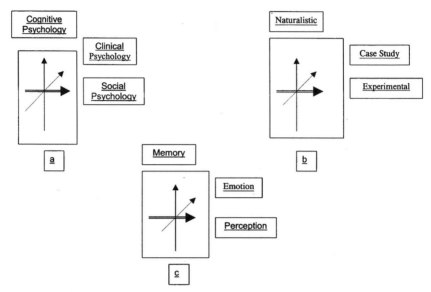

FIGURE 1.1.   Local subspaces for (a) subfields, (b) methods, and (c) mental phenomena in psychology.

The idea is that with enough dimensions, a contribution to a field could be located at a unique point within each of the local subspaces. The dimensions of these local subspaces could be combined into an $m \times n$ space simply by combining the number of dimensions (m) of each local subspace with the number of local subspaces (n), yielding a large-dimensional space. A contribution would then be located at a unique point within the larger space (which might be viewed as a "hyperspace").

If we were to take all of the creative contributions in a given subfield or field or even paradigm at a given time, we could compute the centroid (central point) in the multidimensional space of these various points. This central or most prototypical point, whether computed for a subfield or a field or a paradigm or whatever subset of contributions one desired, would give us the prototype for where a given paradigm, subfield, or field is at a given time. In other words, the centroid represents where a subfield, field, or paradigm is located for the contributors currently in the field. There can be multiple paradigms within a field or subfield at a given time. For the sake of simplicity, we shall refer to a point as representing prototypical work in a given paradigm in a given field at a given time.

A creative contribution represents an attempt to propel a field from wherever it is in the multidimensional space to wherever the creator believes it should go. Thus, creativity is by its nature *propulsive*. It moves a field from some point or region in the multidimensional space to another.

It also always represents an attempt at leadership. The creator tries to bring others to a particular point in the multidimensional creative space. The attempt may or may not succeed.

Eight Kinds of Creative Contributions

The propulsion model suggests eight kinds of contributions that can be made to a field of endeavor at a given time. Although the eight kinds of contributions may differ in the extent of creative contribution they make, the scale of eight kinds presented here is intended as closer to a nominal one than to an ordinal one. There is no fixed a priori way of evaluating *amount* of creativity on the basis of the *kind* of creativity. Certain kinds of creative contributions probably tend, on average, to be greater in amounts of novelty than are others. But creativity also involves quality of work, and the kind of creativity does not make any predictions regarding quality of work.

The panels of Figure 1.2 summarize the eight kinds of contributions and are referred to in the following discussion. For simplicity of representation, the figure is shown in two dimensions, but creative contributions occur in a high-dimensional multidimensional space (whose exact number of dimensions is unknown), as described above. To foreshadow the following discussion—the eight kinds of creative contributions are divided into three major categories, contributions that accept current paradigms, contributions that reject current paradigms, and contributions that synthesize paradigms. There are also subcategories within each of the first two categories: paradigm-preserving contributions that leave the field where it is (1 and 2), paradigm-preserving contributions that move the field forward in the direction it already is going (3 and 4), paradigm-rejecting contributions that move the field in a new direction from an existing or preexisting starting point (5 and 6), and paradigm-rejecting contributions that move the field in a new direction from a new starting point (7). On average, the successive subcategories represent successively more crowd-defying kinds of creative leadership. Consider again the eight kinds of creative contributions, but now with respect to movement in the conceptual space as follows.

A. *Kinds of Creativity that Accept Current Paradigms and Attempt to Extend Them*
   1. *Replication* shows that the field is in the right place. The propulsion keeps the field where it is, rather than moving it. This kind of creativity is represented by stationary motion, such as a wheel that is moving but staying in place.
   2. *Redefinition* redefines where the field is. The current status of the

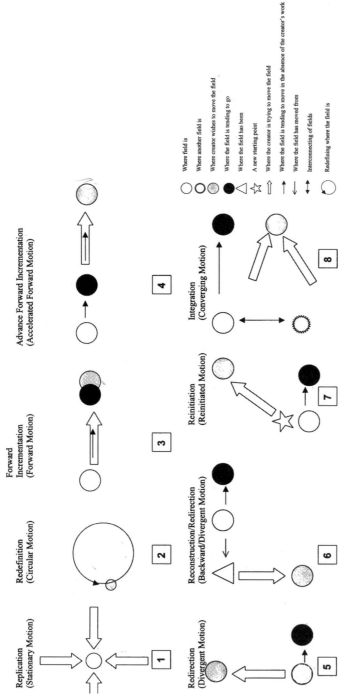

FIGURE 1.2. Kinds of creativity. (1) Replication helps solidify the current state of a field. (2) Redefinition involves a change in perception as to where the field is. (3) Incrementation occurs when a piece of work takes the field from where it is and moves it forward from that point in the space of contributions in the direction the work is already going. (4) Advance incrementation occurs when an idea is "ahead of its time." (5) Redirection involves taking the field from where it is at a given time but attempting to move it in a new direction. (6) Reconstruction/redirection involves moving the field backward to a point it previously was at but then moving in a direction different from that in which it has moved. (7) Reinitiation occurs when a contributor suggests that a field or subfield has reached an undesirable point or has exhausted itself moving in its current direction. The contributor suggests moving in a different direction from a different point in the multidimensional space of contributions. (8) Integration suggests a contributor putting together ideas or kinds of ideas that formerly were seen as distinct and unrelated and even as opposed.

field thus is seen from different points of view. The propulsion leads to circular motion, such that the creative work leads back to where the field is, but as viewed in a different way.

3. *Forward Incrementation* moves the field forward in the direction it already is going. The propulsion leads to forward motion.

4. *Advance Forward Incrementation* moves the field forward in the direction it is already going, but by moving beyond where others are ready for it to go. The propulsion leads to forward motion that is accelerated beyond the expected rate of forward progression.

B. *Kinds of Creativity that Reject Current Paradigms and Attempt to Replace Them*

5. *Redirection* redirects the field from where it is toward a different path. The propulsion thus leads to motion in a direction that diverges from the way the field is currently moving.

6. *Reconstruction/Redirection* returns the field back to where it once was (a reconstruction of the past) so that it may move onward from that point, but in a direction different from the one it took in the past. The propulsion thus leads to motion that is backward and then redirective.

7. *Reinitiation* moves the field to a different as yet unreached starting point and then advances from that point. The propulsion is thus from a new starting point in a direction that is different from that which the field previously had pursued.

C. *Kind of Creativity that Synthesizes Paradigms*

8. *Integration* puts together two types of ideas that previously were seen as unrelated or even as opposed. What formerly were viewed as distinct ideas now are viewed as related and capable of being unified.

The eight kinds of creativity described above are viewed as qualitatively distinct (with the possible exception of forward incrementation and advance forward incrementation). However, within each kind, there can be quantitative differences. For example, a forward incrementation can represent a fairly small step forward, or a substantial leap. A reinitiation can restart a subfield (e.g., the work of Leon Festinger on cognitive dissonance) or an entire field (e.g., the work of Einstein on relativity theory). Thus, the theory distinguishes contributions both qualitatively and quantitatively.

In the discussion below, the various kinds of contributions are exemplified by particular instances from a variety of areas.

Replication

Replication is a form of paradigm-preserving contribution that leaves the field where it is. Replications help solidify the current state of a field. The goal is not to move a field forward so much as to establish that it really is where it is supposed to be. Thus, in science, if a finding is surprising, then a replication can help establish that the finding is a serious one. If the replication fails, then contributors in the field must question whether they are where they have supposed themselves or perhaps have hoped themselves to be. In art or literature, replications essentially show that a style of work can be applied not just to a single artwork or literary work, but to other works as well.

Replications are limiting cases in that they seem, on the surface, to offer the least that is new in terms of the kinds of creative contributions that are considered in this taxonomy. Yet replications are important because they can help either to establish the validity or invalidity of contributions, or the utility or lack of utility of approaches, that have been offered.

When we speak of replication in this chapter, we speak of it broadly in terms of conceptual replications and include small adaptations to existing ideas. We do not refer merely to exact repetitions of what has gone before, which are not creative at all.

In giving examples, we shall here, and in subsequent chapters, divide our examples into three categories: Science and Technology, Arts and Letters, and Popular Culture.

☐ Science and Technology

Consider the choice reaction-time paradigm in psychology as well as its implications. In a choice reaction-time task, a participant presses one of N buttons when one of N lights flashes. In other words, there might be two lights and two buttons, or three lights and three buttons, and so on. Other stimuli besides lights can be used (e.g., two or more tones), but lights are the most common stimulus. As background, Jensen (1982) and others argued that correlations between scores on choice reaction-time tests and scores on intelligence tests suggest that individual differences in human intelligence could be traced to individual differences in velocity of neural conduction. Because tests of choice reaction time in no way measure neural conduction velocity, such interpretations of results were wholly speculative.

Vernon and Mori (1992) tested and seemingly confirmed Jensen's hypothesis. They developed a paradigm whereby they could measure the speed of neural conduction in the arm. They found that neural-conduction velocity did indeed predict scores on conventional tests of intelligence. This was a startling finding because it suggested that what previously had been a speculative claim that at best was very loosely tied to data was instead a serious empirically supported claim. However, Wickett and Vernon (1994) later reported a failure to replicate this result so that its empirical status was cast into doubt. The Wickett and Vernon study was a replication study, and the failure to replicate arguably was as important to the field as would have been a replication. Failures to replicate can prevent a field from pursuing red herrings.

Although work designed to yield exact replications and conceptual replications (where the generality of a finding or kind of product is assessed by trying to replicate it under circumstances somewhat different from those that originally gave rise to it) is often about as unglamorous as any kind of work can be, it is necessary for the development of a field. Without replications the field would be (and probably often is) very susceptible to Type 1 errors (false alarms). In science, replications help ensure the solidity of the base of empirical findings upon which future researchers build. Replications are also important in medicine.

During the twentieth century, Western medicine has rediscovered a therapeutic practice known to the Chinese for 6,000 years. While it may not be a new technique in the broadest sense, acupuncture, the use of needles to relieve pain and cure disease, is a relative newcomer to the repertoire of Western medical practitioners.

There is quite a bit of evidence that acupuncture is deeply rooted in Chinese medicine. Acupuncture needles dating to the first century B.C. have been found in China. Archaeologists have also uncovered a 1026

A.D. manual written by Wang Wei-I, which describes the ancient practice. This text, which set the standard for the method of this ancient art, was inscribed onto clay walls measuring six feet high and 22 feet wide (James & Thorpe, 1994).

Acupuncture is based on the principle that a healthy body is one that retains a balance of energy (Qi). This energy is described as flowing along channels called meridians, which run throughout the body. The practice of inserting needles into key points along the meridians has the effect of restoring the flow of Qi, allowing a natural balance to resume. Techniques of applying needles include varying the angle at which they are inserted and the manner in which they are aggravated (for example, twirled or vibrated) while in position (Singer, 2000).

At one time acupuncture was not even an accepted practice in China. During the Ching Dynasty, from 1644 to 1911, Chinese culture deemed acupuncture too risqué. James and Thorpe (1994) explain that "prudishness increasingly restricted medical practice, as patients considered it immoral to bare their bodies for examination" (p. 42). This sentiment was so pervasive that acupuncture was no longer included in the curriculum at medical schools, beginning in 1822. Given the flow of influence at the end of the twentieth century, it is ironic that, in 1922, the government attempted to make acupuncture illegal. This move was part of their agenda to become more Western. Despite the disappearance of this ancient art, acupuncture was reintroduced in China in 1949 with the rise of communism (James & Thorpe, 1994). Since then, a common variation on acupuncture that was developed in China is the application of electrical impulses to the needles in place of twirling or other manipulation (Singer, 2000).

In recent decades, Western culture, including medicine, has become open to Eastern influence. Western doctors can now elect courses in acupuncture, and many proponents of alternative medicine have reaped its benefits and sung its praise. Numerous researchers are conducting studies to validate the effects of acupuncture, and its effectiveness has been confirmed for the treatment of such problems as the nausea and vomiting caused by chemotherapy (Microsoft, 2000). The mechanism by which acupuncture functions is still unclear even to those who practice it. Theories include those hypothesizing that acupuncture stimulates endorphins, blocks the path of pain signals, and affects the blood vessels, as well as theories that implicate changes in neurotransmitter levels in response to acupuncture treatments (Singer, 2000).

Whether or not Westerners understand quite how it works, Western experience with acupuncture appears to affirm the value of the ancient practice. At this point, the Western application of acupuncture resembles a replication of the Chinese technique. Perhaps the next step in Western acupuncture therapy will be an integration of acupuncture and the administration of drugs. Another future path could involve a forward incrementation that extends or improves upon current acupuncture methods to make them even more effective for treating specific types of ailments. Currently, acupuncture is undergoing a process of redefinition, as medical professionals rediscover the meaning of an ancient Chinese practice as it applies to the field of Western medicine.

☐ Arts and Letters

In the arts and letters, replications help ensure that an approach is robust and can generate a number and variety of works. For example, many artists imitated Monet's Impressionistic techniques, and although they added nothing new to his techniques, they showed the robustness of the techniques for producing varied artwork. Perhaps the limiting case in the art world is the work of forgers, who attempt to reproduce exactly the work of a (usually well known) creator. However, replications are not limited to forgers. Many museum visitors have encountered individuals studiously copying great works of art and proudly displaying their work as copies.

Perhaps the crucial insight for the contributor is to know when there is a need for replication in the first place. In science, this need is associated with findings that are surprising or that seem on the surface to be sufficiently dubious that either their existence or their generality must be demonstrated. In the arts and letters, this need is associated with techniques that may seem to be limited only to a single artwork or artist, or literary work or writer, but that could be used more widely.

Consider an example of replication from the domain of music.

Die Kunst der Fuge (*The Art of the Fugue*), by Johann Sebastian Bach, is an excellent example of conceptually replicatory work that did not revolutionize the field of musical composition but nonetheless is regarded as the ultimate masterpiece in fugal writing due to its high quality. Fugue was a common technique used in musical composition at the end of the Baroque era. Bach's two-volume work, *Das Wohltemperirte Clavier* (*The Well-Tempered Clavier*), includes 48 preludes and fugues in all major and minor keys. In fact, Bach's extensive use of this procedure essentially established the form as a standard in music.

Whereas some composers used the form of the fugue more strictly than did others, distinctive features that characterized the fugal style developed by Bach later came to define this technique in academic music. As Bullivant (1980) explained, "Johann Sebastian Bach is traditionally regarded as representing a culmination of all that had been done in fugal writing" (p. 15).

Die Kunst der Fuge was left incomplete at Bach's death, but the existing manuscript provides enough evidence to demonstrate the magnitude of this undertaking. This piece extends the familiar fugal form to its limit, introducing the basic theme to listeners in each of 24 unique variations. In addition to this first theme, a second was also incorporated into the work, and the manuscript reveals that Bach intended a third. Because of the grand scale and great precision of this work produced by the master of the fugue himself, *Die Kunst* became a standard for Bach's musical followers, engaging the minds of musicians such as Mozart, Schumann, Wagner, Webern, and Berio (Schleuning, 1993). Although Bach did not innovate this technique or even synthesize it with others, there is no question that Bach's treatment and frequent use of the fugal form established it as a versatile and challenging framework for musical composition.

Genre novels and imitative works are also good demonstrations of the replication category. The School of Rembrandt, comprising many different artists who studied with Rembrandt and who tried to create paintings in his style, is an apt example. Another is the novels that were written under the name V. C. Andrews after the novelist died. These were books whose sole purpose was to replicate the feel and style of earlier (and more successful) Andrews books. These works did not advance their respective fields in any substantial way except for reinforcing the initial contributions of Rembrandt and Andrews, respectively.

Replication is not limited to more scholarly domains. It also applies in the domain of popular culture.

☐ Popular Culture

A vintage example of replication can be found in many movie sequels. The creative objective is often not to produce an original work of art, but rather to reproduce the success of the original. In some cases, there may be strings of sequels in a series, such as the *Friday the 13th* or the *Police Academy* movies. These sequels often feature many of the same cast members and a plot similar to the original movie. Not all sequels are replications, however. Some movie sequels (such as *The Godfather, Part 2* or *Superman 2*), while taking the basic plot structure and characters from the original movie, also introduce new concepts and innovative plot twists that make these movies separate entities. Similarly, television movies that are developed from similar sources are often nearly indistinguishable from one another. Perhaps the strongest example of replication in made-for-television movies was when three different movies about Amy Fisher (the "Long Island Lolita" who tried to kill her older lover's wife) aired within weeks of one another.

Another form of replication has been occurring on the Broadway stage.

There are a limited number of sources for creating musical theater, and using a well-known movie as the basis of a musical has always been a popular way both to have an interesting story and benefit from the public's preexisting knowledge of the source material. Musicals that are based on movies (such as *Sunset Boulevard*) are *not* inherently a replication—the basic act of adding original music or rhyming lyrics is a nonreplicative act. But in the late 1990s a new trend emerged—taking a movie that already had music and simply putting it on stage. These types of shows had been sporadically produced in the past (such movies as *Seven Brides for Seven Brothers* and *Singing in the Rain* have been produced on stage), but these productions were not particularly successful and the trend did not immediately catch on.

Footloose and *Saturday Night Fever* were not traditional movie musicals—they contained popular rock music that was not sung by the characters, but rather played in the background. When these two movies were turned into musicals, the predominant goal was to replicate them on stage. The same songs were used, much of the movie dialogue remained intact, and the producers even cast main actors who physically resembled the original stars (an actress named Orfeh, for example, who originated the role of Annette in *Saturday Night Fever* on Broadway, looks strikingly like Donna Pescow, who originated the role in the film). These musicals were able to overcome mostly negative reviews because their core audience was people who had seen the original movies, enjoyed them, and wanted the same experience on a Broadway stage.

Movies can be replicated as musicals, and they can also be replicated as television shows. Some television shows that are based on movies are more than replications, for example, *M*A*S*H*, which benefited from stellar writing, acting, and directing. *M*A*S*H* often looked for ways to stretch the medium of television, such as in one episode that was filmed in real time, with a stopwatch in the lower-left corner of the screen. But most television shows that have their origins in films are only trying to replicate big screen success. Movies as diverse as *Fast Times at Ridgemont High*, *Clerks*, *Working Girl*, *Parenthood*, *Look Who's Talking*, and *A League of Their Own* all have spawned short-lived television shows. Some shows featured actors from the movies; Jon Lovitz, for example, reprised his role as a talent scout in *A League of Their Own*. Other shows had the good fortune to introduce big-name talent—*Working Girl* featured a young Sandra Bullock, and *Parenthood* costarred a preteen Leonardo DiCaprio. But overall, these shows suffered from a lack of inspiration. *Baby Talk* was named as television's worst series in a 1991 critic's poll, while *A League of Their Own* lasted five episodes (Raftery, 2000).

Consumer-goods companies use replication all the time. For example, consider creative replications that can be found on a grocery shelf. Most large supermarket chains offer their own store brand of items. These products are designed to very closely mirror a popular item: A bottle of soda that looks similar to Coca Cola may be called Kola, or a box of cereal with marshmallows and oats that looks similar to Lucky Charms may be given a name like Magic Charms or Lucky Stars. The replications are usually significantly less expensive than the name brand. Similarly, several companies specialize in making generic brands of pharmaceutical goods. These products often use the base ingredients of popular products. They then will often have labels that say, "Compare to the active ingredient in Tylenol!" These products exist for the sole purpose of replicating other companies' success at a lower cost.

Replication can occur in politics as well. A good example of this phenomenon was when George Wallace could not run for governor of Alabama in 1967 because there was a limit to the number of times a politician could seek reelection. Wallace's wife, Lurleen Wallace, ran for governor with a very similar platform to her husband's, and she won the election. George Wallace was named a "special assistant" to the governor, and was symbolically paid a dollar a year to serve in this capacity; as a "special assistant," he consulted and helped Lurleen make many important decisions (Eskin, 1998). Lurleen Wallace's term as governor of Alabama was designed to be a replication of her husband's policies and strategies.

Two different replications can be seen in the evolution of baseball clowning. Al Schacht was the first "clown" on the baseball field. He performed routines before games that spoofed various aspects of baseball (e.g., batting, pitching, etc.). Max Patkin, however, became even more well known by acting similarly for two reasons. First, Patkin was tireless, performing all over the country, and, second, he performed into the age of television and film. As a result, Patkin was immortalized in the movie *Bull Durham*, in which he appears as himself.

Patkin found his calling as a baseball clown in 1944, while serving in the Navy (Crissey, 1999). He performed for more than 50 years (and more than 4,000 games) without missing a performance. While he was originally hired by Bill Veeck to entertain Cleveland Indians fans, he found his home in the minor leagues. Patkin performed nearly an identical routine throughout his career. His acts included the "rock-and-roll pitcher," in which he would pretend to warm up on the mound to the tune of Bill Haley's "Rock around the Clock"; the "water bottle act," in which he drank a large quantity of water and then sprayed it from his mouth; and he imitated every movement of the first baseman as the player warmed up in the infield.

Ted Giannoulas, the original San Diego Chicken, helped pioneer the field of baseball mascots. Taking a partial cue from baseball clowns such as Schacht and Patkin, Giannoulas wore an enormous chicken outfit and performed his routine throughout the game, not only beforehand. Not only did he perform an act or imitate players; he would also actually interact with the players, coaches, managers, and umpires. Giannoulas began his tenure as the San Diego Chicken as a radio station promotion in 1974, handing out Easter eggs in his costume. Soon he was earning a few dollars per hour for walking around the stands at Padres games and entertaining the crowd. Today, no longer limited to San Diego, Giannoulas plays more than 175 events each year (and is paid substantially more than a few dollars an hour!).

With the success of the San Diego Chicken, replications invariably followed. Perhaps the most well known of the subsequent mascots was the Phillie Phanatic. Dave Raymond, the first Phanatic, today runs a school that trains aspiring baseball mascots. Now many professional sports teams have mascots that wear oversized suits in the form of the team nickname (Wallace, 1995).

In sum, replication provides a limiting case of a kind of creative contribution. Another type of contribution occurs when someone proposes not to move ideas forward, but instead views existing ideas in a fresh way. Such a contribution is referred to as redefinition and is discussed in the next chapter.

Redefinition

Redefinition, like replication, changes a field little or not at all. Redefinition involves a change in perception. For example, a navigator may realize that his ship is in a place different from where he thought. Although the location does not change, the definition of where that place is does get altered. Similarly, a redefinition in a conceptual space leads people to realize that the field is not where they had thought. Work of this kind is judged to be creative to the extent that the redefinition of the field is different from the earlier definition (novelty) and to the extent that the redefinition is judged to be plausible or correct (quality). Consider some examples of redefinitions from science and technology.

☐ Science and Technology

Thomson (1939) reinterpreted the work of Spearman (1904, 1927), an English psychologist who invented factor analysis and who used this technique to argue that underlying all tests of mental abilities is a general factor, which he labeled g. In other words, according to Spearman, all important mental abilities ultimately reduce to just a single mental ability, or g. Spearman's analysis had a powerful effect on the field that continues today, with many theorists still believing in the existence and importance of the general factor (e.g., Brand, 1996; Carroll, 1993; Horn, 1994; Jensen, 1998).

Thomson (1939) proposed that although Spearman was correct in asserting a general factor underlying mental tests, he was incorrect in his interpretation of it. According to Thomson, the general factor actually represents the workings of multitudinous "bonds." These bonds are all alleged to be those mental processes that are common to performance on all mental tests. Thus, because all such tests require people to understand the instructions, read the terms of the problems, provide a response, and so forth, there might be many different sources of individual differences shared across these tests. They might appear via factor analysis to be a single entity, but in fact they are multifarious. Thus, Thomson proposed to change not the empirical status of work on intelligence, but how its empirical status was conceptualized. He argued that the field was not where Spearman and others thought it was.

Redefinitions apply in the physical as well as the behavioral sciences. Consider, for example, physics. Quantum mechanics is difficult to understand. Even a famous physics genius, Richard Feynman, claimed not to understand it! And Feynman was not the only physicist who had difficulty fully comprehending the basis and implications of the complex theory. Were experts in the field content to accept quantum mechanics based on faith alone? Feynman certainly was not. Rather than learn by poring over equations and models of the theory, this quirky genius took a different approach to elucidation: He rewrote it! In his doctoral thesis, Feynman applied his own mathematics essentially to re-create all of quantum mechanics.

Feynman's work is a classic case of redefinition—taking a current idea and looking at it from a new perspective. Greenstein (1998) explains that redefining exercises like this one "occupy a time-honored position in science. The game is to do the same thing all over again, but differently. The final result you obtain is nothing new, but you got it in a new and interesting way. As a consequence, you have gained an important insight into what the original result meant. Suddenly, it 'smells' different" (p. 124).

It turned out that Feynman was not the only student of physics who preferred to view the elusive principles of quantum mechanics from this new perspective. His formulation has become a standard in the literature. Although this redefining creative idea did not directly move the field forward, it affected the thinking of future physicists by bringing a complex concept out of the dark into a place where they could see it and really grasp its meaning (Greenstein, 1998).

Redefinitions apply in technological innovation as well as in academic science. Consider a famous example from technology.

Sometimes, redefining the field means seeing a deficit as a potential benefit. Perhaps this strategy—and its serendipitous results—can best be seen in the story of Art Fry, a scientist with the 3M Company. The 3M

Company allowed all of its scientists to spend 15% of their time on personal projects of particular interest to them. Within this encouraging environment, Fry was able to make a most memorable discovery.

Fry sang in his church choir and noticed that whenever he would mark his hymnal with small pieces of paper, these makeshift bookmarks would invariably fall out shortly after they were used. Fry remembered an adhesive that was being developed at 3M that was criticized for not working as well as glue. Perhaps, Fry thought, this supposedly useless adhesive could be used in a new way. He applied the adhesive to a small piece of paper and used it as a bookmark in his hymnbook. It stayed in place, and then it was easily removed without damaging the book. Other uses for the new product quickly became evident, and Post-It notes were soon one of 3M's most profitable products!

☐ Arts and Letters

Redefinitions apply in the arts and letters as well as in science and technology. Consider that even fictional characters can redefine a field. In Thomas Harris's *Silence of the Lambs* (1988), the serial killer Hannibal Lecter was confined to prison for many years. He saw a possibility for escape when he was transferred from his well-guarded prison to a new location. Lecter was watched over by two new guards who did not know the depths of his depravity or ingenuity. Thinking of a way to physically overcome them was comparatively easy for Lecter—the more difficult problem facing him, however, was how to make his escape. He was on the fourth floor of a large building filled with police and FBI agents.

Lecter realized that he had to redefine the whole notion of escape. Rather than try to either sneak out or physically attack the many policemen in the building, he planned to trick them and have them escort him out. Lecter attacked and killed the two guards. He stripped one body and threw it down an elevator shaft. He put on the other dead guard's uniform, fired the guard's gun, and waited. Indeed, the police and the FBI stormed the building, saw what appeared to be a badly injured guard, and summoned an ambulance. Once Lecter was in the ambulance and away from the building, he was easily able to make his final escape (Harris, 1988).

An interesting example of redefinition in the arts is the work of the late Roy Lichtenstein. Lichtenstein took comics, which were viewed as a debased form of art, and turned them into a serious art form. Lichtenstein's work originally met with tremendous opposition, which never really ended, at least in some quarters. Yet in his later career his comic works of art brought extremely large sums of money as well as the kind of serious study that showed what had been perceived as a base art form had come to be taken seriously, at least by many. Andy Warhol is a second example of an artist in this tradition, turning, for example, studies of soda bottles into pieces of art valued by many collectors.

In the world of art, Paul Cezanne "reformulated" the styles of the Impressionists, using the same stroke to paint many different types of objects. He used the style of earlier Impressionists for the purpose of redefining what a painting should be. Cezanne believed that a painting was not a window into the world but an object itself. This theory can be seen in his painting *Still Life with Apples and Oranges* (1895–1900); the fruit do not look lifelike, nor are they necessarily supposed to. In the painting, the table is tilted such that in real life the fruit would probably fall to the floor. But this fact is irrelevant—he was trying to capture the forms and colors of the objects, rather than worrying about his depiction of reality (Hartt, 1993).

☐ Popular Culture

Consider now examples of redefinition in the popular culture. Stage directors who specialize in revivals often excel at redefinition. For example, in the recent Tony Award–winning revival of *Cabaret*, director Sam Mendes reconceptualized the traditionally asexual Emcee as a very sexual—and bisexual—character. Mendes also dramatized the Nazi Germany setting by indicating at the end that the Emcee would be sent to a concentration camp, a decision not in the original script. Although consistent with the character and thematic content of the play, this choice is also a departure from earlier productions that viewed the Emcee as less human.

Another example of redefinition can be found in the recent London revival of *Oklahoma*. The Royal National Theater's Trevor Nunn emphasized the dark side of the traditionally light-hearted musical. Jud, usually portrayed as a pathetic figure, became fearsome and menacing. The ballet sequence in which Laurie chooses between Jud and Curly is foreboding and sexual. Christopher Renshaw is another director who envisioned a usually happy musical as a more serious, intense work. His recent Broadway direction of *The King and I* featured not only a near-dour Anna, but also, in contrast to other revivals, an authentic, all-Asian cast. Although these reconceptualizations certainly enrich the theater, they do not necessarily advance the field. But though the field has not changed (as it would need to for a forward incrementation), the way that people view the field has changed a bit: These stage directors have redefined musical theater as being a more serious and intense art form.

Some common-cultural examples of redefinition are not so cheerful.

One such example is the concentration camp. The prisoners at the Sobibor concentration camp had to be creative when faced with the seemingly insurmountable task of escaping. Previous attempts were few and doomed to failure—the guards were alert and quick to spot someone trying to sneak away. Even if a prisoner was lucky enough to find a moment when the guards were distracted, the communication system was well functioning. Usually within minutes of the escape many guards were looking for the escaped prisoner, and the person was usually caught quickly and subsequently executed.

The leaders of the Sobibor escape, however, redefined the problem. Instead of seeing escape from the death camp as something involving hiding or running, they conceptualized escape as an aggressive act. One of the leaders was a Russian soldier who was able to incorporate battle tactics in planning the escape. The prisoners waited until they could attack the Nazis one by one. One Nazi, for example, was killed while trying on his new boots; another was killed while inspecting the kitchen. The prisoners then took the guns from the dead bodies and were able to kill enough of the guards at the gate to get through. They also cut the phone wires, so the guards were unable to immediately call for back-up help. Eluding gunshots and mines, more than 300 prisoners escaped from the camp that day. Several of them are still alive (Rashke, 1987).

Redefining a field does not have to be a life-and-death matter, however. In Game Three of the 1972 World Series, the Athletics (A's) were holding onto a tight 1–0 lead over the Reds. Future Hall-of-Famer Rollie Fingers was on the mound, pitching to another fellow future Hall-of-Famer, catcher Johnny Bench. There were runners on second and third bases, and only one out. The game—and the series—was on the line for the A's. If Bench connected for a base hit, the Reds would be in a good position to win the game. If he made an out but made contact (either a ground ball or a fly ball), then the score might be tied. If, however, Bench struck out, then the A's would have the clear advantage.

Fingers worked the count to 3-and-2, and the A's then-manager Dick Williams went to the mound for a conference. There he redefined the problem. Rather than making Bench swing and miss (and therefore strike out), what if Fingers could get Bench to not swing at all? Williams decided to fool Bench into thinking that the A's were going to walk him. As the manager walked back to the dugout, he pointed to first base and nodded, as though he were telling Fingers to intentionally walk Bench. Then Williams pointed to Tony Perez, the batter in the on-deck circle, and nodded again, with the implication being that they would face Perez.

A's catcher, Gene Tenace, stood up and held his glove to the side of the plate, indicating he was expecting a ball. Fingers nodded and motioned his head to the side, as though indicating that he was going to intentionally throw the ball out of the strike zone so that Bench would get on base. With such an elaborate set-up, Bench assumed that he was going to be walked, and he relaxed. Fingers then promptly threw the ball straight down the middle, Tenace hopped back into his position and caught it, and Bench was stuck staring at strike three. The threat of a big inning was quelled, and the A's held on to win the game by a score of 1–0. They then proceeded to win the World Series (*Fastball*, 1999).

Redefinition applies to video games as well. Video games have become an integral part of American culture. Just as the invention of the television in the 1950s redefined entertainment and indirectly influenced many arenas of American life, the introduction of the video game in the 1970s has initiated a change in the nature of childhood play throughout society.

Where did video games come from? Who first had the idea to make television interactive, to give people the power to control the action on the screen? The origins can found in one of the first video games, Pong. Video games actually stem from a very simple concept invented in the 1950s by an unsuspecting physicist working at Brookhaven National Laboratories in Upton, New York, Willy Higinbotham.

Higinbotham's original "video game" was designed to add some spice to a public tour of his instrumentation laboratory. Because Brookhaven was involved in nuclear research, these tours were organized to show visitors that the research was entirely peaceful and posed no risk to residents. Higinbotham knew that the tour of the facility was not very exciting, so he tooled around with an oscilloscope and a simple computer, built a few controls with buttons and knobs, and created what can be considered the first video game. The game was conceptually very similar to Pong: One player presses a button to launch a ball from the left side of the screen, adjusts a knob so the ball clears a barrier in the middle of the screen, and a second player hits the ball back over the "net." With these modest beginnings, the video game industry was born.

Little did Higinbotham know that his simple tennis game would not only relieve boredom on the tour of his laboratory, but that players would form lines, eager to try their hand at the novel challenge. Before Higinbotham understood the potential of the demand he had created, marketers seized the idea. In fact, Pong is simply a redefinition of Higinbotham's basic tennis game. The originators of Pong did not seriously revamp the design, but they did bring to it a new perspective. Realizing the game's potential for fascination (and remuneration), they grabbed their opportunity to latch onto the public's interest. As almost every American child can attest, their fascination has not waned, and the video game industry continues to profit (Flatow, 1992).

Redefinition also applies in the food industry. In one case, a split-second decision represented an attempt to redefine a field. Jeno Paulucci was a businessman who had just purchased Chun King, a canned food company. Paulucci wanted to use this company to sell his own food inventions, Cantonese vegetables with Italian spices. Paulucci met with the main buyer for a top food chain to try to sell his Chun King cans to be distributed by this chain. If the businessman was able to make the sale, his company would surely take off and become profitable; if not, it would be a difficult task to maintain financial solvency.

Demonstrating his product, Paulucci opened a can of chop suey vegetables and saw a cooked grasshopper sitting right in the middle of the can. Paulucci had one brief moment in which the grasshopper was hidden from the buyer by the open can lid. What could he do? If the buyer saw the grasshopper, the sale would surely not go through, and Chun King's reputation would likely suffer. Think about what you might do in such a situation.

In those few seconds, Paulucci redefined the role of a salesman from a passive role to a very active role. A typical businessperson might have either tried to surreptitiously remove the grasshopper from the can (and run a high risk of being caught) or tried to explain the many legitimate reasons why the dead grasshopper was not indicative of his or her company's product. Paulucci decided to attempt neither of these strategies. Instead, he looked the buyer in the eye and said that the vegetables looked so good that he wanted to have the first bite himself. Paulucci took a large forkful of vegetables, including the fateful grasshopper, and ate with a big smile. He got the sale (Hay, 1988).

Sometimes, a redefinition of the field means reevaluating traditional roles. A psychiatrist saw a patient who said that he was beginning to doubt his sanity. The patient said that he believed that the stock market was going to crash, and he obsessed about it. All of his friends kept buying and thought that his concerns were ridiculous, so the man agreed to get professional help. The psychiatrist saw the man for five sessions, at which point he told his patient that he could not determine anything wrong with his sanity—his logical processes were sound and his thoughts did not seem delusional. The next day, the man and the psychiatrist stepped out of their traditional roles and both started selling their stocks. The year was 1928. The man was Charles Merrill, whose ability to completely survive the stock market crash helped establish his firm Merrill Lynch (Gordon, 1999).

The redefinition of a field may occur and yet not be made public until years later. In 1921, Frederick R. Barnard, the advertising manager of Street Railways Advertising, used the phrase, "One look is worth a thousand words" in an ad he placed in *Printers' Ink* in 1921. He attributed the saying to a "famous Japanese philosopher." The adage was refined into "One picture is worth ten thousand words" in another Barnard ad six years later, attributed as an ancient Chinese proverb. This quote eventually became a part of the lexicon and often has been presented as a Confucian saying.

Barnard, however, had subtly redefined the field of advertising. The public respects philosophers more than advertisers. Barnard coined the expression himself but decided to attribute it to an ancient philosopher to make it more impressive. Barnard's subterfuge remained a secret for many years until uncovered by Burton Stevenson (Safire, 1996).

In a similar vein, Wall Street speculator Jay Gould's redefinition of the field of speculation did not arise until his objective had been reached. The minister of his local church asked him for investment advice, and Gould advised him—in confidence—to purchase shares of Missouri Pacific. The minister thanked him for the advice and invested in the stock, which, after a brief rise, plummeted and bottomed out. The minister lost nearly everything. When the minister told his troubles to Gould, the speculator instantly wrote him a check for the full amount lost. The minister then admitted that although Gould's advice had been in confidence, he had told many of the other members of his congregation. Gould's manipulations then became known. "I had a feeling that would happen," he told the minister. "Those were the people I was after" (Hay, 1988). Gould redefined the field of speculation. He was able to reach people and through a source—their minister—that would be much more trusted than he would have been. By banking on the minister's inability to keep a secret, Gould made a great deal of money.

A similar redefinition can be found in the actions of the treasurer of the New York Philharmonic Society. When many years ago, the treasurer asked philanthropist Andrew Carnegie for money to pay off the Philharmonic's debt, Carnegie initially agreed, but then hesitated. Not wanting to pay the entire debt himself (to encourage the Philharmonic to learn other ways of raising money), he said that he would happily pay half of the debt if the Philharmonic could find a matching donor for the other half of the money. The debt was substantial (approximately $60,000), and finding another donor for such a large sum of money was not an easy task. But the treasurer was able to redefine the idea of fundraising, and he thought of an untapped resource. Indeed, the next day the treasurer told Carnegie that he had found the matching funds. Carnegie was pleased, and the philanthropist asked the name of the other contributor. "Mrs. Carnegie," the treasurer said (Hay, 1988).

Redefining a field can help win elections. In 1874, Grover Cleveland had an illegitimate son with a young widow. The boy was subsequently put up for adoption. When Cleveland ran for president 10 years later, it provided fodder for his Republican opponent, James Blaine. Blaine made Cleveland's illegitimate child a large issue in the campaign, and Blaine's follower's chanted "Ma, Ma, where's my Pa?" (Eskin, 1998). They also spread rumors that if Cleveland was elected, he would bring many young women with him to Washington.

Before public sentiment could turn against Cleveland, he and his advisors redefined the field of campaigning. In addition to being completely honest about it (a bit of a novelty right there), they also reshaped the question. Cleveland admitted to fathering the child, but then he (or his advisors) put a brilliant spin the issue. Several ethical questions had been raised about whether Blaine had received illicit money from a railroad company. Although Cleveland had admittedly behaved questionably in his private life, Blaine had not; on the other hand, Blaine may have behaved questionably as a public official, while Cleveland's reputation was more secure. The proper response, Cleveland's followers suggested, would be for Cleveland to be sent to the White House to be a public servant, while Blaine should be restored to his rightful role as a private citizen. Cleveland's rare honesty—and redefinition of the situation—helped secure his victory as president (Boller, 1984). Indeed, Cleveland's win gave the Democrats a punchline to the Republican slogan: "Ma, ma, where's my pa? Gone to the White House, ha-ha-ha!"

In sum, redefinition involves taking a phenomenon that people see in one way and looking at it in another way. Basically, one stays with phenomena that already are givens. In forward incrementation, considered in the next chapter, one moves on to new phenomena.

CHAPTER

Forward Incrementation

Forward incrementation occurs when a piece of work takes the field at the point where it is and moves it forward from that point in the space of contributions in the direction work is already going. There is no change in the trajectory of the field. Work of this type is judged to be creative to the extent that it seems to move the field forward from where it is and to the extent that the movement appears to be correct or desirable. Forward incrementation probably comes closest to what Kuhn (1970) referred to as "normal science." Martindale (1990) has written of a similar kind of contribution in the arts.

☐ Science and Technolology

Consider an example of forward incrementation in psychology. Hunt, Frost, and Lunneborg (1973) proposed that investigators could study intelligence by examining individual differences in cognitive performance on the kinds of tasks cognitive psychologists study in their laboratories. These tasks included, for example, how quickly one could identify whether two letters viewed on a computer (or other) screen were the same letter (e.g., *A* and *a* are the same letter). A few years later, Hunt, Lunneborg, and Lewis (1975) published an incrementation study that extended the range of tasks that could be studied using this paradigm, and that suggested that certain tasks were particularly useful for studying individual differences in verbal ability. The second study was an incrementation study, building on a paradigm that Hunt and his colleagues already had established. The second study provided a fairly substantial increment in both increasing the range of tasks and in focusing in particular on verbal ability.

Most studies published in scientific journals can be characterized as forward incrementations. For example, after the initial groundbreaking study of Festinger and Carlsmith (1959) on cognitive dissonance, in which it was discovered that people who lied to others preferred a smaller reward for lying rather than a larger reward for lying (so that they could then lie to themselves about why they were lying!), huge numbers of follow-up studies were done on phenomena of cognitive dissonance and cognitive consistency (Abelson et al., 1968). These studies helped elucidate the phenomenon and its limiting circumstances. As these forward incrementations clarified the limits of the cognitive-dissonance phenomenon, other theories were proposed that provided alternative (Bem, 1967) or more refined explanations of when people exhibit cognitive dissonance or other reactions—such as self-perception—in the face of cognitive inconsistencies (Fazio, Zanna, & Cooper, 1977). The self-perception interpretation was that people who lie to others prefer a smaller to a larger reward not to resolve the uncomfortable feeling that the lying has created, but because they come to perceive themselves in a different way from the way they did before they lied.

Examples of forward incrementations can also be found in technological innovation. The invention of the incandescent lamp is a good example of the forward incrementation typical of step-by-step progress in normal science and technology (Kuhn, 1970). Although Americans strongly associate the name Thomas Edison (1847–1931) with the invention of the light bulb, Joseph Swan (1828–1914) of England deserves equal scientific credit for his work on the problem, as do many others who also contributed small steps along the way toward the successful product.

The first attempts at creating a light bulb can be traced to 1838, when Jobart "sealed a carbon rod inside a vacuum and watched it glow as a current was passed through it" (Clark, 1985, p. 220). By 1847, the concept of an evacuated bulb with a carbon filament was solidified. But specific problems remained. Incandescent lamps in the mid-1800s burned for a very short time due a combination of two factors. First, the filaments were not durable, and, second, there was too much air inside the bulb (Yarwood, 1983).

As the technology was not yet available to create a vacuum inside the bulb, experiments focused on perfecting the filament. Swan experimented with a carbon filament treated in various ways, whereas Edison believed that a platinum filament was the answer. In 1865, Hermann Sprengel introduced the mercury vacuum pump, and 14 years later Edison acquired such a vacuum pump and met success with a carbon filament (Clark, 1985).

Step by step, scientists settled on the carbon filament and began to produce light bulbs in quantity by 1882. At that point, the only impediment to more widespread use of the bulbs was the lack of electrical wiring in homes and businesses. The next step of the path was cleared as Edison and his colleagues set out to create a system of electricity to bring power to cities. Even after Thomas Edison and Joseph Swan joined forces to create United Electric Company, experiments on metal filaments continued (Yarwood, 1983). Eventually, the tungsten filament became preferred because of its high melting point, and it remains the standard in the light bulbs of today.

Whereas some discoveries are characterized by distinct moments of insight that create a discontinuous path of progress, the light bulb is better viewed as the product of a scientific evolution directed by careful experimentation and simple trial and error. Such forward steps or incrementations are key to the progress of every scientific field.

Another example of a next step in science, this time in medicine, is Pasteur's development of vaccine therapy following his germ theory of disease. After the germ theory had described a mechanism for the cause of disease, the next step was to extend the theory's implications for disease prevention, namely, vaccine therapy. The concept of vaccination did not originate with Pasteur (nor did pregerm theory advances in sanitary practices in medical settings). Edward Jenner had earlier discovered the effectiveness of using small amounts of cowpox to vaccinate humans against small pox (Meadows, 1987).

Pasteur reasoned that the administration of similarly attenuated germs might prevent the development of bacterially caused diseases. His first attempt, using fowl cholera, proved a success. Although at first he did not realize that the attenuation was caused by prolonged exposure to warm air, later experiments with anthrax in cattle confirmed that time and heat did indeed sufficiently weaken the bacteria. Pasteur's great triumph of vaccine therapy was in a dire case of a young boy attacked by a rabid dog. After administering a culture developed from the brains of dogs and rabbits, the boy's survival was celebrated and the miraculous effectiveness of vaccination assured (Meadows, 1987).

Vaccine therapy was not a new idea to Pasteur, in that Jenner had already used it in the treatment of smallpox. In fact, ancient Chinese culture had already recognized this technique in the tenth century. Alchemists in China administered a smallpox vaccine by inserting slightly infected plugs of cotton into the noses of healthy individuals. But Pasteur extended this method to include new diseases caused by germs he had identified, the logical next step, an increment forward on a path well chosen.

☐ Arts and Letters

Forward incrementations can also be found in the arts and letters, such as in genre fiction that pushes the envelope. The hard-boiled detective story pioneered by Dashiell Hammett and Raymond Chandler has been elaborated upon by countless writers, some of them moving the genre forward in major ways, such as Ross MacDonald, who introduced identity confusions as a major theme in his work. But MacDonald's work and that of others has its roots in the paradigm introduced by Hammett and Chandler.

Jonathan Kellerman's psychological thrillers take the genre a step further by having the hero, Alex Delaware, actually be a clinical psychologist. Patricia Cornwell's suspense novels have Kay Scarpetta, a medical examiner, as the protagonist. Using these nonstandard professions instead of the usual cops and detectives adds an extra layer of authenticity to the stories and allows for much more technical detail to be added to the plots. Kellerman's plots, for example, often hinge on Delaware identifying various psychological syndromes (for example, Munchausen Syndrome by Proxy), while Cornwell has Scarpetta discover essential clues in her autopsies. The forward incrementations also can be found in the plots of genre fiction. Agatha Christie's classic *The Murder of Roger Ackroyd* (1926) is a fairly standard murder mystery, until the then-startling ending that reveals the narrator is the killer. These advances certainly move the field forward, but in an expected, nonstartling way. Kellerman and Cornwell still work within the preestablished conventions of the field, and Christie's famed novel still obeyed most of the "rules" of a murder mystery.

Forward incrementations can occur in the classical arts as well, of course. The futurist painters began a movement that rose up in opposition to romanticism. Futurism, unlike many other artistic movements, was drawn to speed and noise and embraced technology; it was also drawn to fascism (*Futurism*, 2001). The futurist painters, such as Carlo Carra and Umberto Boccioni, infused these political ideas into their cubist-schooled art. Their art reflected the power of an industrial state, and the presence of the fascist ideas conveyed extra meaning to the preexisting style of cubism (Hartt, 1993). In photography, Diane Arbus moved away from more commercial work (photographing celebrities and other members of the elite) and began to explore in the 1960s a wide variety of subjects. The people she photographed were from out-groups of society who were rarely photographed, such as the mentally handicapped, the physically disabled, nudists, and transvestites. And yet Arbus's photographs, rather than mocking or singling out her subjects, were compassionate and nonjudgmental. Her ability to capture these people on film and allow them humanity paved the way for many other photographers who would specialize in undervalued or unusual individuals (Bosworth, 1995; Hartt, 1993).

☐ Popular Culture

In the popular culture, quality genre television shows often use forward incrementations to stand apart from their predecessors. Shows such as *Hill Street Blues* and *L.A. Law* advanced the concept of the "law" or "cop" shows from the tradition of *Dragnet* and *The Defenders* to incorporate aspects of characters' personal lives. In addition to chasing criminals or defending clients, these lawyers and policemen fell in love, endured the loss of a parent or friend, and sometimes had important "outside" interests, all of which were as central to the plots as the actual cases. Other shows such as *E.R.* and *NYPD Blue* push the envelope further, using violence and gore to further illustrate their characters' professional lives, and sex and nudity in their characters' private lives. Part of this forward incrementation is a result of reduced censorship, but part is also due to the creative powers of such series creators and writers as Stephen Bochco and David E. Kelley (Brooks & Marsh, 1995).

Vaudeville and live performance frequently feature forward incrementation in the succession of new and varied acts. When entertainer Herbert Brooks developed a routine of being able to produce from his coat pockets—without looking—any playing card an audience requested, Arthur Lloyd did him one better and extended the trick to any card—a club membership card, a business card, a sporting event ticket, a marriage license, and so on. Lloyd's coat filled with cards had more than 40 pockets, weighed up to 100 pounds, and contained approximately 15,000 items (Jay, 1986). Similarly, London entertainer Ethardo specialized in balancing on a ball and then rolling *up* a spiral track. But, again, LaRoche took the trick one step further and fit himself *inside* the metal ball. The sight of the metal sphere seemingly moving by itself up a long spiral incline was even more astounding to spectators than the earlier acts (Jay, 1986).

Forward incrementation applies to the Internet as well as to television. Several of the top websites on the Internet are the result of forward incrementations. From the 1990s to the present day, an entrepreneur could find a business that worked in the "real world" and then apply it to an on-line site. In the early days of the web, it could be as simple as deciding that an Internet bookstore could offer a nearly infinite selection of books, because there was no need actually to have the books physically present in one location. Sites such as Amazon.com (www.amazon.com) attest to the wisdom of such a decision. Other sites applied a similar rubric to auction houses (eBay, www.ebay.com), music stores (CDNow, www.cdnow.com, among many others), and outlet stores (OutletBound, www.outletbound.com). By now, most of the obvious venues have been used on the Internet, so it would likely take even more than a solid forward incrementation to develop a successful and innovative website.

An example of forward incrementation can also be found in the financial solicitation of the Hare Krishnas. Like many other religious groups, the Hare Krishnas met with little interest when they solicited donations from passersby; most people tend to donate money only to their own religious groups, or to those with which they feel a connection. The Hare Krishnas advanced their money solicitation technique to a new level by adding a measure of social psychology—the principle of reciprocity. This principle states that when a person gives you something, you feel dutybound to return the favor (Cialdini, 1984). The Hare Krishnas began handing out flowers to people—as a "gift"—and then asking for money. Having accepted the flowers, people then felt bound to reciprocate and give the Hare Krishnas a donation. With the forward incrementation, the Hare Krishnas were able to collect a great deal more money than they had previously been collecting.

Forward incrementations can even be found in the now out-of-fashion "freak shows." Today, growths and even extra appendages can be removed fairly easily in a doctor's office. Even an extremely large "extra" body part can be handled surgically. But 200 or even 100 years ago, these extra limbs were permanent. A circus promoter like P. T. Barnum often paid very enticing salaries for these individuals to allow themselves to be put on display. One obvious way to attract more customers was to treat the growth as a separate entity—often the "extra" limbs were given names. Sometimes they were even dressed in clothing and called a miniature twin. The managers of Laloo went a step further, taking the field of "freak show" display a forward incrementation further. Laloo had a large growth attached to his breastplate that appeared to be a miniature person from the waist down. Laloo's managers decided that one way to get even more people to enter their show was to dress the growth in female clothing and claim it was a woman! Indeed, Laloo became a very popular attraction (Drimmler, 1973).

A series of forward incrementations can be seen in the history of breast enhancement. In nineteenth-century Paris, the Bust Improver was sold. The Bust Improver was a bodice fitted with woolen pads; these pads gave the appearance of a larger bust. The Bust Improver was a forward increment over the earlier, less reliable method of hand-stuffing the bodice with rags, paper, or cloth. A few years later, another increment occurred when the pads were developed with rubber. By the 1890s, another increment changed the marketplace when the "breast pad harness" was introduced. This device consisted of padded artificial breasts attached to elastic straps. By the 1930s, plastic pouches were being used instead of rubber; these pouches were usually filled with water or oil (Panati, 1989).

The next significant forward incrementation was developed during World War II in Japan. Prostitutes who catered to American soldiers realized that the soldiers preferred large-busted women—and would pay more for them. The Japanese prostitutes began arranging for doctors to inject a variety of liquids into their breasts in order to make them larger; these liquids ranged from a saline solution to goat milk to, finally, liquid silicone. By 1962, the phenomenon had moved to America, where two plastic surgeons implanted gel bags filled with silicone into young women. This type of surgery remained popular until a variety of apparent health hazards mostly ended this procedure (Panati, 1989).

Breast enhancement, of course, is designed to enhance overall beauty. Forward incrementations can also be seen in our popular ideals of beauty, in general. By the turn of the century, the ideal woman possessed European features and Victorian moralities. But Charles Gibson, an artist and illustrator for *Life*, began drawing pictures of women that were dubbed Gibson Girls. Stunningly beautiful, with dark hair and hourglass figures, the Gibson Girls usually wore blouses and skirts—an indication of their liberation and self-confidence (Panati, 1991). The Gibson Girl sensation quickly spread across America. Men were in love with the image, women wanted to resemble the image, and other countries often assumed that this ideal was actually what the average American woman looked like.

The Gibson Girl became so popular, in fact, that the drawing of the man with whom she was often pictured became popular in its own right. The Gibson Man, as he was called, was perhaps most notable for being clean shaven in a time when a mustache and beard were considered distinguished; the popularity of the Gibson Man began to reverse this perception. The Gibson Girl was eventually usurped in popularity by other ideals of beauty (such as the vamp and the flapper), but the image still surfaces today as a symbol of turn-of-the-century appearances. Gibson was adept at merchandising and licensing the drawing, and he became a wealthy man. His forward incrementation of Americanizing the standard ideal of beauty was a very profitable one (Panati, 1991).

Forward incrementation applies in politics as well as in ideals of beauty! Congressman James E. Watson gave the field of booking political speakers a forward incrementation and killed two birds with one stone by doing so. Watson, a Republican from Newcastle, Indiana, was worried that his party was losing the support of the African American vote. He was also worried that a local Civil War hero, General Lew Wallace, was lessening his involvement with the party. If Watson wanted to win reelection, he needed the support of both Wallace and the African American voters.

So Watson decided to invite Ben Tillman, a senator from South Carolina, to talk at a large town meeting in the early 1900s, giving Tillman free rein to talk about whatever topic he liked. Tillman accepted the engagement and chose to talk about African Americans. Tillman was an outspoken racist and still a supporter of the Confederate cause. Tillman ripped into the Republican party for "coddling" African Americans. Not surprisingly, this tirade produced a very negative reaction in the crowd. But this same crowd made sure to show up to spite Tillman's racism and vote Republican. General Wallace, meanwhile, was appalled that the Republicans would be reduced to having such a speaker. Wallace re-signed with the party, agreeing to give speeches at a number of fund raisers and meetings—perhaps so that Tillman would not be invited again! Watson's idea of adding reverse psychology to his scheduling of political speakers was a most rewarding forward incrementation, as he was reelected (Boller, 1991).

Theodore Green, a Democratic senator from Rhode Island, also used reverse psychology as a forward incrementation in his campaigning. After he had taken a taxi with a friend and paid the driver, Green told his friend that the driver was a guaranteed vote in his favor. The friend was puzzled—had Green given a large tip and told the driver to vote Democrat? No, Green said, he did not tip at all, and told the driver to vote Republican (Boller, 1991)!

A forward incrementation that occurs often arises (as with Congressman Watson) from a desperate situation. Harold Knutson ran for Congress as a Republican from Minnesota in 1916. The other candidate had a great deal of money to run a thorough campaign, while Knutson had very little. But Knutson had a creative idea that represented a forward incrementation from standard campaigning. The prospective congressman altered his car so that he could disable the carburetor, or do something similar that would make the car stop. Knutson would cause the car to stop when he saw a prospective voter, and then politely ask for help in fixing the car. The prospective voter would usually easily be able to get the car running again (there was not anything truly wrong with it in the first place!), and Knutson would thank him and strike up a conversation. Knutson would then mention that he was running for Congress before leaving to find another prospective voter. Knutson rode his "broken" car all the way to an election (Boller, 1991).

Incumbent Democratic Senator Claude Pepper was the victim of a dirty political campaign in 1950 that would certainly qualify as a forward incrementation. If campaigning as a field has advanced to include "dirty" and "below-the-belt" campaigning, then his opponent, George Smathers took this forward incrementation one step beyond. Smathers did not just campaign dirty by banking on the public's prurient nature and interest in mud slinging, he also counted on the public's basic ignorance.

Smathers's campaigns assumed that the public would not understand the true meanings of long complicated words (especially words that sound naughty), so they said things like, "Claude Pepper is known all over Washington as a shameless extrovert." The ads also accused Pepper of practicing "nepotism" with his sister, who was once a "thespian." Pepper also, the ads said, practiced "celibacy" before he was married. As Smathers had predicted, the people who read these ads assumed that the words they did not know represented illicit and immoral things. Smathers won the primary election over the incumbent Pepper, mostly because of a correctly aimed (if not particularly nice) forward incrementation (Boller, 1991).

Forward incrementation also applies in the sports arena. When the salary structure in baseball began to go higher and higher in the 1980s, the various teams approached the issue in different ways. Some teams invested all of their money in one huge deal for a superstar player. Other teams signed many good players to one-year deals, banking on a championship team that year. But the Cleveland Indians took an old strategy and modified it, and, in the process, created a dynasty for the 1990s. In the late 1970s, the Kansas City Royals signed some of their best players (such as George Brett) to long-term deals. These contracts were often for more years than the players could reasonably play, but it was a gamble. If the players stayed healthy and productive, then their per-year salary would be a bargain. If not, then the Royals would suffer. As it turned out, Brett and the other players maintained a high level of play, and the Royals became one of the few small-market teams to be competitive in the mid-1980s. The Royals had the luxury, however, of dealing with salaries that were still somewhat reasonable—the Indians had no such luxury. The Indians' actions represented a forward incrementation in baseball management. They picked out several of their very young players who were in their first, second, or third year. These players, many of whom were not well established, were willing to sign long-term deals for less money (although still much more money than a young player would usually get). The Indians' gamble paid off, and many of the young players (such as Jim Thome, Manny Ramirez, and Omar Vizquel) developed into stars (or, at least, solid players). Because they acted quickly and boldly, the Indians were able to sign the core of their team for several years, and they went on to be a perennial winner in the late 1990s and beyond.

Another forward incrementation can be seen in a hatter's gamble. When

P. T. Barnum auctioned off the first ticket to a concert of Jenny Lind (a singer known as the Swedish Nightingale), an obscure hatter named Genin saw the makings of a business opportunity. He bid $225—a very large amount of money at that time—and waited for the public reaction. As he had anticipated, people were surprised by the high bid, and they talked about it. Nobody had heard of Genin. Yet with newspapers and the telegraph, millions of people soon read about the hatter who paid so much money for a ticket to see Jenny Lind. People became curious to find out more about Genin, and in the process they learned about his hats. He sold ten thousand extra hats each year for the next several years and established his company as a successful one—all rooted in a forward incrementation of a publicity scheme (Hay, 1988).

A very different type of advertising campaign represented a forward incrementation not only as a method of raising awareness of a product, but also as an approach to traffic safety and guidance. The Auto Club of Southern California (currently known as AAA) decided in 1913 to place road signs that gave traffic and directional information. These signs were placed on the roads that ran from Kansas City to Los Angeles. These signs served an important function for motorists, because in 1913 maps were often unreliable and cross-country travel was a difficult undertaking. Signs that guided a driver safely to his end destination were necessary (and, indeed, the federal government would eventually take responsibility for this task). But in addition to providing a service, the signs served as a smart advertising campaign—the Auto Club's name became well known to the very group of people it was trying to reach: automobile owners, many of whom were new residents of Southern California. The Auto Club used their road signs to take advantage of a remarkable growth spurt in Los Angeles in the 1920s (the population of Los Angeles more than doubled during this decade), and this technique established their organization to become the largest regional AAA affiliate, with nearly five million members (Johnson, 2000).

In sum, forward incrementation is creative by virtue of taking existing ideas and moving them one step or, at most, a small number of steps forward. Sometimes, though, people move things many steps forward, perhaps beyond where their audience is ready to go. In such cases, we deal with advance forward incrementations, as discussed in the next chapter.

Advance Forward Incrementation

Advance forward incrementation occurs when an idea is "ahead of its time." Although the field is moving in a certain direction, it is not yet ready to reach a given point. Someone has an idea that leads to that point not yet ready to be reached. The person pursues the idea and produces a work. Often the value of the work is not recognized at the time because the field has not yet reached the point where the contribution of the new work can be adequately understood. The creator accelerates beyond where others in his or her field are ready to go—often "skipping" a step that others will need to take. The value of the work may be recognized later than otherwise would be the case, or some other creator who has the idea at a more opportune time may receive credit for the idea.

There are probably few innovators who seek to create advance forward incrementations. Much more likely, the innovators produced what they thought would be a reasonable next step (forward incrementation) in thinking, only to discover that they were ahead of their time—the public was not ready for their innovation.

☐ Science and Technology

Consider an example of advance forward incrementation in psychology. Alfred Binet is best known for his work on intelligence, but, as pointed out by Siegler (1992), Binet also examined the nature of expertise in outstanding chess playing and the validity of eyewitness testimony. The work, which did not fit even remotely into existing paradigms of the time, was largely ignored. By the second half of the twentieth century, these and other topics that Binet had studied gained prominence. Binet, however, is virtually never cited in the current work on these topics.

Royer (1971) published an article that was an information-processing analysis of the digit-symbol task on the Wechsler Adult Intelligence Scale (WAIS). In this task, one is given a legend that matches digits with corresponding symbols. Each time one sees the digit, one then has to draw the corresponding symbol. The task is strictly timed, so that the main issue is how fast one can match the digits to the corresponding symbols. In his article, Royer showed how information-processing analysis could be used to decompose performance on the task and understand the elementary information processes underlying the performance. In other words, what mental steps did people take in solving the digit-symbol problems? Royer's work foreshadowed the later work of Hunt (Hunt, Frost, & Lunneborg, 1973; Hunt, Lunneborg, & Lewis, 1975) and especially of Sternberg (1977, 1983), but his work went largely (although not completely) unnoticed. There could be any number of reasons for this, but one of the reasons is likely to have been that the field was not quite ready for Royer's contribution. The field and possibly even Royer himself did not recognize fully the value of the approach he was taking.

Sometimes, advance forward incrementations not only drive their audience crazy, but their proposers as well. In the nineteenth century, Ignaz Semmelweis, a Hungarian obstetrician, proposed the idea of microorganisms contaminating the hands of doctors and was so scoffed at that eventually he became mentally unbalanced. Often it is only later that the value of such works is appreciated.

Many of the same ideas apply in other domains. Consider, for example, the domain of computers. According to Cardwell (1994), "If anyone was born out of his time it was Babbage; his ideas about the computer were only to find their rightful place by the middle years of the twentieth century" (p. 420).

In 1834, a British mathematician named Charles Babbage (1791–1871) envisioned the universal computer. Just over a century before the first modern computers were created, Babbage wrote up plans for a powerful analytical engine that had the capacity to perform diverse and complex functions. Babbage's analytical engine was a mechanical computer, complete with a memory store and the ability to operate conditional logic. Input and output were recorded in binary code on familiar punch cards. Although many engineers and scientists in the nineteenth century knew of Babbage's work, they did not pursue the potential of his ideas. They simply were not ready. Thus, Babbage's creative contribution can be viewed as an advanced forward incrementation.

The uniqueness of this example is not merely in its precocity, but also in its original emphasis on pure science. Whereas Babbage had hoped to create a universal computer, the demand for computers in businesses and the military did not require the flexibility of a universal engine, but instead was focused on creating specialized machines. The first computers that emerged around the turn of the twentieth century thus were business machines. One well-known early computer was Hermann Hollerith's business machine, which was designed to aid in calculating the census of 1890. During the wars, great progress was made in creating specialized computers that could make pointed calculations related to battle. Such computers were powerful but suffered from severely limited memories. For example, in order for such a computer to change its specialty, it had to be completely reprogrammed, a process that required parts of the computer to be modified and the machine rebuilt.

The concept of a universal computer, however, was not lost among scientists whose orientations were more basic. While computers were being developed to estimate ballistics during World War II, German engineer Konrad Zuse was aiming to create a universal computer, a scientific machine with great flexibility and less specificity. By 1941, he had built his Z3 computer. It was a mechanical universal machine that performed various tasks at the command of computer programs. Around the same time, from 1939 to 1944, International Business Machines (IBM) built a scientific universal computer according to specifications set out by Howard Aitken of Harvard University. This machine was entirely mechanical, stretching 50 feet long and run by a four-horsepower motor. Although the first IBM computer did not have the capability of using conditional logic, its creators could be proud of their success in carrying out Babbage's vision of an analytical engine whose purpose was purely scientific.

In fact, British mathematician Alan Turing took Babbage's concept of a universal computer to a hypothetical extreme with his invention of what has become known as the Turing machine. This machine exists only in an abstract sense, but it was instrumental in Turing's essay "On Computable Numbers, with an Application to the *Entscheidungsproblem*," proving that numbers existed whose precise value could not be computed.

Computers have had a revolutionary impact on many areas of modern life, from the first business machines to today's miniature hand-held day planners. Charles Babbage's notion of the universal machine came a century before the first machines were built, a prototypical example of an idea ahead of its time. Perhaps the demands of the day dictated the path of progress on computer development, but Babbage's universal analytical engine was bound to return to the fore once the conditions were right. Incidentally, the revolution that has followed the advent of the computer age would not have been a surprise to the one who was there at its conception. Babbage has been quoted as predicting that "as soon as an analytical engine exists, it will necessarily guide the future course of science" (Cardwell, 1994, p. 483).

Although not a century ahead of its time, Michael Faraday's field theory of magnetism, like Babbage's computer, did not become an accepted part of the field until its validity was proven by scientists some 40 years after it was originally proposed.

In the early nineteenth century, scientists were fascinated with understanding the relationship between magnetism and electricity. Michael Faraday (1791–1867) was a British chemist who had also become intrigued with the relationship between these two physical phenomena. In 1821, Faraday demonstrated that not only can electric current act like a magnet, but that magnets can induce electrical current. Faraday's contributions to this line of investigation included the invention of several instruments, such as the electric motor, the electrical transformer, and the dynamo, devices that demonstrated the conversion of magnetism to electricity and of electricity to mechanical motion (Meadows, 1987).

Common theorizing about magnetic forces considered magnetism to be similar to gravity. Just as two bodies are attracted to one another, more or less depending on their distance from each other, two magnetic bodies also possess an amount of attraction. The strength of the attraction between two objects was thought to be a direct function of the distance between them. However, Faraday focused precisely on this distance, proposing that the space between two magnetic or electric objects was not uniform, but rather was composed of "lines of force." These are the lines observed in the textbook example showing the position of iron filings in the vicinity of two magnets. Faraday's field theory held that magnetic forces acted as fields between objects rather than as forces that lay within the objects themselves (Meadows, 1987).

Acceptance of this view of magnetism would necessitate a fundamental shift in scientific understanding at the time. Unfortunately, his contemporaries did not appreciate the import of Faraday's field theory. These contemporaries were not satisfied with the theory and awaited a mathematical proof of it. The scientific world waited for this proof until 1873, when Scottish physicist James Clerk Maxwell (1831–1879) published his *Treatise on Electricity and Magnetism*. This work not only proved the validity of Faraday's field theory, but also confirmed another prediction of Faraday's, which stated that light is actually a kind of electromagnetic wave (Meadows, 1987). Finally, the foresight of a great chemist was validated.

☐ Arts and Letters

In the arts and letters, an advance forward incrementation is a work whose potential typically is not realized at its premiere, yet is later recognized as a step along the historical path of a genre, and is often considered a work ahead of its time. Perhaps the most memorable premiere in music history is that of Igor Stravinsky's ballet *The Rite of Spring* in 1913. This performance of music and dance so shocked its Parisian audience that the instrumentalists could not hear themselves play over the riotous crowd. At the time, French ballet music was very backward looking and accompanied a very stylized choreography. Of course, the usual ballet patrons were bound to be overwhelmed by the enactment of barbaric rituals accented by pulsating rhythms and dissonant harmonies featured in Stravinsky's new work.

Although the premiere of *The Rite* was vehemently rejected, Stravinsky's innovation was rooted in the past and proved to be an important step in the future course of music history. The pressing and irregular rhythms of ritual in this work continued the rhythmic experimentation begun by Stravinsky's teacher, Nikolai Rimsky-Korsakov. This deemphasis of melody and harmony is also characteristic of works later in the century. Just as Stravinsky borrowed elements from folk music for this piece, many twentieth-century composers also made extensive use of nonart music sources in their compositions. Although *The Rite* was poorly received at its premiere, its contribution to the field of music can be considered simply ahead of its time (Machlis, 1979).

Advance forward incrementations occur in art as well as in music. The painter Kasimir Malevich, by contrast, received more appreciation when his works premiered. In 1912, he painted *Knife Grinder*, an abstract series of multicolored geometric shapes that came together to form the image of a knife grinder. His 1918 *Suprematist Composition: White on White*, a diagonal white square on a white background, moves beyond postimpressionism and is "very nearly the ultimate in abstraction" (Hartt, 1993, p. 988). His new and innovative style, which he dubbed suprematism, was noted for its geometric abstraction and became quite influential later in the 1920s.

Consider a literary example of an advance forward incrementation. A literary technique that became especially popular in the 1980s was the advanced forward incrementation of "writing back" against the classics. While similar at first glance to the "sequels" to literary classics (see Chapter 7, Reconstruction/Redirection), these works took themes, characters, or plots from classic works of literature or history and examined them from a radically different point of view. Jean Rhys's *Wide Sargasso Sea* (1966) is a novel about the first Mrs. Rochester. In its source material, Charlotte Bronte's *Jane Eyre*, Rochester sweeps Jane off her feet, and his first wife surfaces only as a lunatic who is mostly used as a plot point. Rhys, however, centers her entire book on the first Mrs. Rochester, probing at the reasons behind her madness.

Roberto Fernandez Retamar's *Caliban* (1989) is an essay that takes the point of view of Prospero's unhappy creation. While Shakespeare's play *The Tempest* views Caliban as a deformed savage, Fernandez Retamar grants him humanity. Michael Dorris and Louise Erdrich's *Crown of Columbus* (1991) tells the story of a Native American woman and her husband following Columbus's diary in search of supposed treasure. As in the works by Rhys and Fernandez Retamar, those of Dorris and Erdrich focus on an oppressed person who has previously been seen only as a footnote to history. All of these works use modern values and ideas to "write back" against past values, many of which were racist and sexist. By presenting a minor, undervalued character as the protagonist of a new work, it offers the chance to both accept the character as important in his or her own right, as well as an opportunity to reevaluate the original work.

These works anticipated the wave of political consciousness (or, as it sometimes is called, "correctness") that has pervaded much of the arts in recent years. Rhys's novel, for example, did not sell very well when it first was published, yet it was rereleased some years later to much more acclaim. Fernandez Retamar, as well as Dorris and Erdrich, received a respectful but underwhelming critical reception when their works were published, but perhaps their work, too, will be reevaluated in the future as the field continues to evolve.

☐ Popular Culture

Advance forward incrementations have a place in the popular culture, such as in the world of film. Making film biographies of creative artists has long represented a successful formula. A forward incrementation was to use the works of these artists as a focal point of a movie (such as the use of Gershwin's music in *Rhapsody in Blue* or Van Gogh's paintings in *Lust for Life*). But two movies showed an advance forward incrementation by not merely incorporating an artist's work, but also telling a fictional story of the artist's life that blends their life and works. Steven Soderburgh's *Kafka*, starring Jeremy Irons in the title role, does purport to tell the story of Kafka—and, indeed, the main character is a man named Franz Kafka who works at an office job by day and writes by night. But what the movie does that represents an advance forward incrementation is tell a Kafka-esque story involving conspiracies, subterfuge, surreal situations, and paranoia. The end product is a blend of a Kafka story and a Kafka biography. Like many advance forward incrementations, *Kafka* was a bit ahead of its time and did not receive particularly good reviews. Another film that was released several years later perfected the technique.

The Oscar-winning *Shakespeare in Love* took this similar tactic and used it to create a much more successful film, for which people were ready. The basic story of the movie is imagining how William Shakespeare might have written his classic tragedy *Romeo and Juliet*. As in many stories about writers, the film cleverly shows where he may have received his inspiration. Shakespeare has a lover early in the movie named Rosaline, with whom he then grows disenchanted, much as Romeo grows disenchanted with his early love Rosaline. Shakespeare walks by a preacher who says (in reference to the two theaters of the day), "A pox on both their houses," much as Mercutio will later recite in *Romeo and Juliet*.

But *Shakespeare in Love* does something that is brilliant that advances the field of film biography. While Shakespeare is writing his famous play, his life begins to resemble a typical Shakespearean play. He first meets his eventual lover when she is dressed as a boy, auditioning for one of his plays. And, indeed, she gets the role—of Romeo. His adventures of writing the play and falling in love are filled with such Shakespearean devices of gender switching, mistaken identities, bawdy humor, wild plot turns, and royal influence. By the time the movie is over, the audience has not merely *seen* a Shakespearean story, they have *lived* through one.

Musicals can also provide examples of advance forward incrementations. Many of Stephen Sondheim's musicals in the 1960s, 1970s, and early 1980s were examples of advance forward incrementations. Sondheim had experienced mainstream popular success both as the lyricist of *West Side Story* and *Gypsy* and for writing both music and lyrics for the Broadway hit *A Funny Thing Happened on the Way to the Forum*. But he still struggled and was generally underappreciated. Most people associated *West Side Story* and *Gypsy* with their composers (Leonard Bernstein and Jules Styne, respectively), and Sondheim's score to *Forum* was widely attacked (and did not receive a Tony Award nomination, even though the show picked up six Tony Awards, including Best Musical!) (Suskin, 1990).

His musicals from the 1960s to today represent an advance forward incrementation of the field and were not adequately appreciated at the time they were written; it is only in the last decade or so, as his current work receives more and more acclaim, that his earlier contributions have earned more notice. Sondheim's lyrics were absolutely brilliant examples of rhyme and rhythm; no one since the days of Cole Porter could write lyrics (for example) such as "In the depths of her interior/Were fears she was inferior/and something even eerier/But no one dared to query her/superior exterior." This lyric has six rhymes woven into a single verse. Yet not only does it make sense, it does not seem awkward.

The lyrics, however, were from *Follies*, which lost the backer's money despite running for more than 500 performances. And *Follies* was one of his most successful post-*Forum* shows; *Anyone Can Whistle* ran for nine performances, losing money; *Merrily We Roll Along* ran for 16 performances and lost money; *Pacific Overtures* ran for 193 performances and lost money. *Company* and *A Little Night Music* were more successful, but even these shows did not rank as Broadway's biggest hits at the time. Yet while other musicals that were originally more successful are rarely revived (such as Tony award winner *Two Gentleman of Verona*), these shows are very often revived. A concert version of *Anyone Can Whistle* brought out some of Broadway's best talent (including Madeline Kahn, Angela Lansbury, and Bernadette Peters), while a popular version of *Merrily We Roll Along* played off-Broadway in the mid-1990s (Suskin, 1997).

Sondheim pushed the field ahead with the brilliant lyrics and, most importantly, his mature "nonmusical" themes. *Follies* is about regret; *Company* is about a young man wondering earnestly if he will ever be ready to commit to marriage; and *A Little Night Music*, whose songs are all written in waltz time, takes an adult approach to issues of marital fidelity and loyalty. Sondheim advanced the field beyond the point that it was able to accommodate and in doing so he confused and annoyed many theatergoers who were hoping for either the light entertainment of the past or the rock opera musicals of that day. Sondheim was a serious playwright who dealt with human emotions and characters, yet chose the musical as his art form (Zadan, 1989). Luckily, Sondheim has lived long enough (while keeping active) to see his older work resurface and be reexplored and rediscovered. Many creators of works of advance forward incrementation do not have this luxury.

Entertainment is not limited to movies and musicals, of course. Comedians also provide entertainment. A comedian whose whole career consisted of advance forward incrementations was the late Andy Kaufman. When he began in the 1970s, most comedians saw their primary purpose as that of entertainment. Some comedians took entertainment a step forward, and they tried to be challenging, thought-provoking, or controversial. Kaufman took his mission in comedy a step beyond this goal, and aimed at a much different audience reaction—confusion, frustration, and sometimes even anger. Kaufman's career was filled with so many different types of advance forward incrementations in comedy that it would be impossible to summarize them all; here are a few of his most memorable ones.

His first major television appearance was on the first episode of *Saturday Night Live*. While the show tried very hard to be different—and often succeeded—it was Kaufman who was *so* different that many people in the audience had no idea what he was doing. He played a record: the theme from *Mighty Mouse* ("Here I come to save the day . . . "). He didn't sing along at all throughout the entire first verse; he just stood, waited, and grinned. As the chorus played, Kaufman gustily mouthed along to the words, and then returned to being quiet during the verses, waiting for the chorus to be played again. Many people in the audience thought this was truly original (and very funny), while others were simply confused (Zehme, 1999).

Throughout his career, Kaufman tried to be unpredictable and different. No matter how far the field advanced, he always wanted to push it in new directions. He developed a routine of being "Foreign Man," in which he spoke in a disoriented, jumbled accent that was vaguely European. This routine became popular, and he played a version of this character on the television show *Taxi*. Once the public accepted "Foreign Man," however, he stopped enjoying it. During one stand-up performance, in which the crowd was yelling at him to perform as "Foreign Man," he took out a copy of F. Scott Fitzgerald's *The Great Gatsby* and began reading from it. The crowd waited for the joke, but there was none coming. Kaufman read the entire book out loud to the crowd until two o'clock in the morning (at which point there were very few people left to be read to). Perhaps this example shows that not all advance forward incrementations are necessarily good ones.

Kaufman was fascinated with wrestling. Later in his career, he proclaimed himself the champion of intergender wrestling and offered a lot of money to any woman who could beat him wrestling. He was challenged by a popular wrestler (Jerry Lawler) and they had a loud, public fight that landed Kaufman in the hospital—except it was all faked, and Lawler was part of the joke (unbeknownst to the public). Most people did not realize that it was all an act and thought Kaufman's misogynist, elitist speeches were reflective of his actual beliefs. They were not (Zmuda & Hansen, 1999).

When Kaufman was diagnosed with cancer in his thirties, people thought it was another joke. He did not smoke, and yet he said he had lung cancer. As he got sicker, fans would still approach him in his wheelchair and punch him on the shoulder, telling him to stand up and stop fooling around. He died at the age of 35 in 1984. His lasting legacy, however, was the way that the field of comedy eventually caught up with his advance forward incrementations—current superstars such as Robin Williams and Jim Carrey (who portrayed Kaufman in *Man on the Moon*) cite him as a major influence, and many of his ideas about the blending of hype, fantasy, and reality can be seen in everything from television trash talk shows to parodies of documentaries (Zmuda & Hansen, 1999).

Some achievements that we take for granted today represented advance forward incrementations when they began. In the 1930s, when America was mired in the Great Depression, Michael Cullen's ideas changed the way that most people do their shopping: He saw a need for lower food prices. At that time, the predominant way that people bought food was through Mom-and-Pop grocery stores. These stores, however, were both slow (clerks filled customers' orders, resulting in long lines) and somewhat expensive (the quantities of food that the Mom-and-Pop stores could purchase were not large enough to give them discounts). Cullen also noted that there were several other factors in place that made a new idea possible; most notable of these factors was the automobile, which enabled people to be able to travel farther to purchase food (Panati, 1991).

What Cullen did was to advance the field of food purchasing—and, by extension, shopping—drastically: He opened the first supermarket. Cullen opened huge stores that stocked enormous quantities of food. He chose low-rent locations that were not in the center of town. Yet they were locations that were suddenly accessible because of the automobile. Cullen even set aside paved lots for shoppers to park their cars, an innovation by itself. He invented the art of balancing prices: By making a profit on one product, he could sell another product at cost. These bargains went a long way in attracting a large audience for the new supermarket. He also introduced an early version of the shopping cart (an improvement over baskets). In addition, Cullen borrowed (from a different chain of stores) the idea of self-service, which helped cut down on his overhead (Panati, 1991).

Unlike many others who introduced advance forward incrementation, Cullen's creation was immensely—and immediately—successful. One reason for this success was that while the field was not ready for his creation, the public was. Mom-and-Pop grocers tried to convince the government to make Cullen's price cutting illegal. They also tried to persuade newspapers not to accept advertisements for supermarkets. But the Great Depression had created a public that was eager to save money in any way possible, and the objections of the other grocers meant little. Indeed, many other supermarkets soon opened in competition with Cullen's stores (Panati, 1991).

In sum, advance forward incrementations carry a field beyond where most of the audience in that field is ready to go. Nevertheless, advance forward incrementations are not paradigm rejecting. Redirections, considered in the next chapter, are paradigm rejecting.

CHAPTER 6

Redirection

Redirection is a form of creative contribution that is paradigm rejecting. Redirecting contributions move the field in new directions from existing or preexisting starting points. Work of this type is creative to the extent that it moves a field in a new direction (novelty) and to the extent that this direction is seen as desirable for research (quality). Consider some examples from science and technology.

☐ Science and Technology

In their pioneering article mentioned earlier, Hunt, Frost, and Lunneborg (1973) wrote that researchers of intelligence use cognitive-psychological paradigms in order to study intelligence. The basic idea was to correlate scores on cognitive tasks with scores on psychometric tests. Sternberg (1977) used cognitive techniques as a starting point, but suggested that research move in a direction different from that offered by Hunt. In particular, he suggested that complex cognitive tasks (such as analogies and classifications) be used instead of simple cognitive tasks (such as lexical access—that is, retrieving names of letters from memory) and that the goal should be to decompose information processing of these tasks into its elementary information-processing components. Sternberg agreed with Hunt regarding using cognitive tasks, but disagreed with using very simple ones, which he believed involved only fairly low levels of intelligent thought. Sternberg was thus suggesting a redirection in the kind of cognitive work Hunt had initiated.

An earlier and more important example of a redirection can be found in the work of the psychologist Edward Tolman. Tolman (1932) made an effort to redirect the field of learning, an endeavour that today has earned Tolman a place in virtually every serious textbook on learning or even on introductory psychology. Tolman accepted many of the conventions of the day—experiments with rats, use of mazes, and multitrial laboratory learning experiments. But he proposed to take all of these features of research in a new direction, one that would allow for purposiveness and latent learning on the part of the animals he was studying. Today, of course, these concepts are widely accepted, although at the time Tolman proposed them, the reaction was mixed, at best.

Redirections also apply in the field of physics. $E = mc^2$ is a formula most people associate with the off-the-charts genius of Albert Einstein. In fact, Einstein's special theory of relativity is a great creative contribution to the field of physics. Specifically, its impact yanked the field a full 90 degrees from its previous trajectory into an exciting and challenging new direction.

It all started with Einstein's fascination with light. In the nineteenth century, Maxwell determined that light was a kind of electromagnetic wave. This notion led to the logical assumption that light waves travel through a medium much like ocean waves travel through water. Seventeenth-century scientists referred to this sea of light as the "ether." When Newton proposed his theories of motion, the ether was the key to the measurement of absolute motion. Whereas all motion seems to be relative, comparison to the ether could yield a measure of absolute motion. Convenient as this concept was, nineteenth-century scientists failed to detect the existence of the ether in any of their experiments on the nature of light (Meadows, 1987).

Einstein was troubled by this inconsistency and concentrated on the problem of light. Using thought experiments, Einstein realized that light waves travel at such a high rate of speed that they are essentially insurmountable. If light travels faster than anything else, then that speed can be viewed as an upper limit, a kind of constant. A constant? If the speed of light is constant, and all other motion is relative to that constant, then suddenly the problem of the ether becomes irrelevant. Einstein concluded that absolute motion need not be measured relative to some elusive, cosmic ether, but rather relative to the constant of the speed of light.

Einstein published his conclusion in 1905, the theory that is now referred to as his special theory of relativity. This theory was a redirection in science. Until 1905, scientists assumed that relative motions were perpetually relative because there was no absolute against which to compare them. However, Einstein's theory eliminated this problem with its parsimonious explanation of the natural constant, light. This discovery forced the field to view relative motion from a new perspective, despite sometimes-counterintuitive predictions of this new perspective.

What may surprise those outside the field of physics is that another scientist who had been working on relativity problems had actually come to conclusions very similar to Einstein's. Hendrik Lorentz (1853–1928) had recently developed formulas describing the relativity of the dimensions of moving objects when viewed by a person who is standing still (Cohen, 1985; Meadows, 1987). But Einstein went well beyond Lorentz in his theorizing. Einstein's theory later was further investigated by such esteemed physicists as Max Planck, Max Born, and Hermann Minkowski. All acknowledged that Einstein's theory was a breakthrough. Minkowski reworked Einstein's mathematics into the form that is commonly accepted today (Cohen, 1985).

It is without question that Einstein's new ideas about light and relativity resulted in a sharp turn on the path of physics research as it entered the twentieth century. In fact, some might expect that this revolutionary theory should qualify as a reinitiating contribution. It is true that Einstein's discovery overturned some principles of Newtonian mechanics, but his thoughts did originate within the tradition of normal physics. Cohen (1985) quotes the 1911 Nobel Prize winner in physics, Wilhelm Wien, as saying that Lorentz may have been the first to formulate the "mathematical content of the relativity principle"; however, Einstein "succeeded in reducing it to a simple principle" (p. 412). A true reinitiation rejects fundamental principles of the current field, but the continuity of Einstein's ideas with the ideas of others such as Lorentz confirms that his breakthrough theory is best viewed as a redirection in the field.

Another redirection occurred in telecommunications with the invention of the telephone in 1876. During the nineteenth century, people communicated with one another over long distances using the revolutionary telegraph network. However, as the technique became more popular, supply could no longer meet demand. The problem was that only one message could travel over a given wire at any given time, and there simply were not enough wires to carry all the messages that people wanted to send. In 1872, the race was on to find a way to send more than one message simultaneously over the same wire (Flatow, 1992).

Alexander Bell (1847–1922), a teacher who enjoyed tinkering, believed he might have a solution to this problem. Based on his experience with tuning forks, Bell reasoned that it might be possible to send two messages over the same wire if they caused the wire to vibrate at different frequencies. He experimented with tuning-fork transmitters set at different pitches and receivers in the form of reeds set to vibrate at the same frequency as the tuning forks. Once Bell was able to tune the reeds to resonate with the forks, he was able to show that his hypothesis was correct: Each fork caused a response in its respective reed, and the two frequencies did not interfere with each other! This was Bell's harmonic telegraph (Flatow, 1992).

Follow-up experiments with his new musical instrument revealed that when the tuning fork was plucked, its tone was transmitted to the receiver. Bell's suspicions that speech could be transmitted similarly over wire were beginning to become plausible. Bell knew that he only needed a transmitter that could convert speech into electrical signals, and the telephone then could become a reality. Meanwhile, Elisha Gray, a successful inventor, had been working on the same telegraph problem, and had come to similar conclusions. However, Gray was discouraged by businessmen and others who believed that the telephone would never be profitable. Unfortunately, Gray listened to the shortsighted businessmen, and his design of the telephone was set aside (Flatow, 1992).

This is the point where Bell's daring to defy the crowd paid off. Bell's recent breakthrough with the harmonic telegraph propelled him forward. Flatow (1992) writes, "Bell could no longer ignore [opportunity's] knock. He would give up on the telegraph and concentrate on the telephone" (p. 81). Rather than follow the path of normal science, working to perfect the telegraph system, Bell saw an opportunity to make a new contribution, one that could redirect the field toward a communication system based not on dits and dahs, but rather on the authentic human voice.

The rest of the story is well known. Bell patented his telephone in 1876, just hours before Gray's application arrived at the patent office (Flatow, 1992). That Bell received credit is an example of how, in science and technology, being just a little bit too late can cost one the credit one might otherwise have earned. A few years later, the invention of the microphone by David Hughes (1831–1900) greatly improved the quality of telephone communication, and spurred its more widespread use. The first telephone lines were installed shortly thereafter in 1878 in New Haven, Connecticut. By the 1920s telephones had become a standard mode of communication (Williams, 1987). Although the telegraph did not immediately fall into disuse, the addition of the telephone pushed our communicative repertoire in a new direction. Today, telephones are sophisticated and adaptable.

An invention that had redirective effects on the field of communication as well as on the wider social and intellectual world is the printing press with movable type. The first printed book dates to ninth-century China, although the printing press did not appear in Europe until the mid fifteenth century. Whether these developments were independent or related is of less concern than is the impact of the printed word on society at the time of its introduction.

Prior to the invention of movable type and the printing press, books were laboriously copied by hand. For this reason, books were rare and precious. When Johannes Gutenberg (1394/99–1467) introduced the concept of movable type in 1448 in Mainz, Germany, a revolution followed. Especially in Europe, the 26-letter alphabet was particularly well suited to the use of movable type. Any book could be reproduced by mixing and matching many multiples of these 26 basic prototypes. (This was not the case in China. Given the large numbers of characters used in the Chinese language, movable type was simply not as practical in China as it turned out to be in Europe [Cardwell, 1994]). It has been estimated that there were more books published in Europe between 1450 and 1500 than had been published in the previous 1,000 years (Yarwood, 1983).

The immediate and lasting effect of Gutenberg's contribution can be summarized as the grand facilitation of the dissemination of ideas. Gutenberg's process affected many aspects of culture, including the dissemination of information about religion.

Perhaps the best-known printed volume associated with Gutenberg's name is his version of the Latin Bible. As a case in point, greater public access directly to scripture had revolutionary (or, at least, reformatory) effects on the culture at the time. As bibles became more available, lay people who were not proficient in Latin wished to read the text in their native language. As vernacular bibles became available, the theology of the Church was also in a parallel transition. Martin Luther (1483–1546) advocated direct access to the scripture by lay people, preaching a new Reformation theology that argued for a direct and personal relationship with God (Rubenstein, 2000).

One of the most popular products of early presses was the indulgence, a certificate that could be purchased from the Catholic Church in exchange for an absolution of sins. Appropriately, the presses also helped disseminate the famous 95 theses against the sale of indulgences first posted by Martin Luther in 1517. Although such heretical theological ideas would normally have been discussed among Luther's colleagues at the university in Wittenberg, the printed versions of his theses no doubt spread his controversial ideas to others, perhaps gaining subtle support for his call for reform.

Rubenstein (2000) interprets the scientific revolution as an indirect result of the new technology of the printing press. The dissemination of scientific ideas through print eliminated the obstacles set up by the many geographical boundaries that had previously existed between researchers working on similar problems. Moreover, the increased availability of books allowed ambitious individuals to educate themselves, thereby reducing the gap between the peasants and the property owners in the Renaissance.

The invention of the printing press greatly facilitated the spread of ideas in an age of great progress. From the careful molding and casting of movable metal type to the printing and binding of the illustrative Gutenberg Bibles, the printing press has been pivotal in redirecting the history of European culture.

☐ Arts and Letters

Redirections occur in the arts and letters as well as in science and technology. Consider the work of Beethoven, whose compositions can also be viewed as a redirection from the classical style of music that had been employed so successfully by Haydn, Mozart, and others. Beethoven used many of the same classical forms as had his predecessors. But he also showed that a greater level of emotionality could be introduced into the music without sacrificing the classical forms.

Some musical redirections are more contemporary. A composer who is well known for his stated attempt to redirect the field of music in the early twentieth century is Arnold Schoenberg. Schoenberg may be best known for his rejection of tonality, though he wrote extensively on the continuity of his musical ideas with the past. Schoenberg viewed tonality as a means of organizing musical materials; his position was that there are other means for providing organization to sound, and his 12-tone method was an example of that means. In taking this position, the composer was attempting to direct the rest of the musical community toward a higher art with less emphasis on comprehensibility for the masses and more emphasis on progress among experts (Stein, 1975).

Schoenberg's aim was not to write radical and atonal music, but to make use of a challenging new structural format in his compositions. His first piece that employed the 12-tone method entirely was his *Suite for Piano*, Op. 25 (1924). A true witness to his claim that this new musical language could express any musical style, Schoenberg wrote a suite similar to those typical of the early eighteenth century (consisting of six movements in song and dance forms). Despite the lack of traditional tonal harmonies, Schoenberg's work uses traditional forms and rhythms. The piece includes a prelude with Bach-like counterpoint, an intermezzo reminiscent of Brahms, as well as a classical minuet in the sonata form made standard by Mozart and Haydn.

The romantic pieces of late nineteenth century challenged the rules of harmony by changing tonality often. Schoenberg took things one step beyond this weakened tonality and declared all tones of the scale of equal importance. In doing so, Schoenberg believed he was founding a new Viennese school of composition, which would ensure the dominance of German music into the twentieth century. Despite the loyalty and musical refinements of his disciples, Alban Berg and Anton Webern, Schoenberg's 12-tone method became the regular compositional model for few notable twentieth-century composers (Machlis, 1979).

Redirections apply in literature as well as in music. Kurt Vonnegut's classic *Slaughterhouse Five* (1969) and Tim O'Brien's (1990) *The Things They Carried* tried to redirect the field of war novels, not just by adding new dimensions to the form but by questioning the goals and the reality of the form. Vonnegut's prologue to his story of the hapless soldier Billy Pilgrim includes a conversation in which someone accuses him (Vonnegut) of glorifying war by writing a war novel. Any war novel, the character says, even the ones that say "war is hell," end up glorifying war. Vonnegut promises not to do this and, indeed, does not. Pilgrim is not a noble or heroic character—he is pathetic and passive. And Pilgrim's mental undoing is not described or hinted at—it is graphically and *physically* portrayed in his capture by an alien race, the Tralfalmadorians, who have a philosophy that smacks dangerously of repression and other defense mechanisms.

O'Brien questions the truth of war and all war stories. His central character is a writer named Tim O'Brien who fought in the Vietnam War, and his book is written in the first person. In real life, O'Brien did fight in the Vietnam War. Is it a true story? How much is fact and how much is fiction? O'Brien does not tell. "Let me tell you a true war story," he writes, and then he describes how he killed a man during the war. "But no," he says, "that is not true; here is the truth." And then O'Brien tells an entirely different story of how he killed someone during the war. "You know what," he then writes, "that was not true, either." His point is that the "details" of war do not matter—what are important are the central themes and emotions. The reader can, presumably, infer that at some point, in some manner, O'Brien killed a man, but who knows?

Vonnegut questioned the very fabric of what constitutes a war novel, and in doing so forged a path for the future of the field. Re-creations and straightforward stories of the horrors of war (such as Stephen Crane's *The Red Badge of Courage* or MacKinlay Kantor's *Andersonville*) are powerful, Vonnegut might argue, but to truly convey the nature of war an author must go beyond this. O'Brien picks up on Vonnegut's path and takes it in yet another direction: An author *cannot* convey the nature of war to someone who has not experienced it. All he or she can do is convey the feelings and thoughts one might have in these types of situations. O'Brien and Vonnegut are not reinitiators, as they are accepting the same starting point for war novels that other novelists have used. Their work is also not merely a type of forward incrementation, however, because they have taken a radically different view of the way in which a war novel should be written.

☐ Popular Culture

Redirection can be found in contemporary rap music as well as in more traditional kinds of music. Early rap music was urban and did not appeal to a mainstream audience. The group Run-DMC, however, redirected the field toward a different audience. Rather than aiming for the same audience to whom the early rap music played, Run-DMC tried to reach a wider group of people. They added guitar riffs and more melody to their songs to make the rap songs sound more like more mainstream rock and roll. They collaborated with famous rock bands such as Aerosmith (for the hit song "Walk this Way"), and as a result appealed to an entire audience (Aerosmith's many fans) that might otherwise not have been inclined to listen to rap music. Run-DMC became extremely successful and was the first rap group to attain breakout mainstream popularity (Light, 1999).

Consider the idea of redirection as it applies in a very different domain, in particular, in banking. In 1822, a clerk, M. Labouchére, worked for the banking firm of Hope & Company in Amsterdam. He was sent to London to try to obtain a loan from a prominent banker named Baring. Labouchére proceeded to redirect the current rules concerning both negotiation and wooing—and in the process, he not only was able to get a loan, but he also drastically changed his life.

In the process of discussing the loan, Labouchére got to know Baring's daughter and became smitten. He asked Baring for her hand in marriage, and was quickly rebuffed—the upper-class Baring would never let his daughter marry a clerk. Labouchére asked if his chances would be improved if he were a partner at Hope & Company instead of a clerk. Baring agreed that if Labouchére did, indeed, become a partner, then he would have Baring's permission to marry his daughter.

Labouchére then returned to Amsterdam and asked his boss, Mr. Hope, about becoming a partner. Hope quickly said no, pointing out (correctly) that Labouchére did not have his own fortune (and, by extension, the proper background for the job). Labouchére then asked, "What if I was married to Mr. Baring's daughter?" Hope agreed that if Labouchére was Baring's son-in-law, the situation would be different, and he would be named partner.

With these two promises firmly committed, Labouchére returned to London, and two months later was married to Miss Baring (Hay, 1988).

Labouchére obtained firm promises from important people, and he saw a way to redirect the field away from the more standard ways that transactions are usually carried out. Because of his creativity, Labouchére was rewarded with a plum job and marriage into a powerful family.

Redirection also applies in marketing. Redirecting the concept of advertising children's toys saved Mattel from going out of business in the 1930s. The toy company, which was years away from making Barbie Dolls, was close to bankruptcy, but made the wise decision to invest nearly all of its assets in the sponsorship of television's *The Mickey Mouse Club* (Panati, 1991). Mattel took existing advertising strategies and redirected them. In the past, toy companies had tried hardest to sell their products to wholesalers and store buyers; if the toy store buyers did not choose to stock a particular toy in the store, then it was not sold. If the toy companies were going to target any public audience, it would be parents (Stern & Schoenhaus, 1990). But by sponsoring *The Mickey Mouse Club*, Mattel reached children directly. Mattel's new Burp Gun was advertised on the show, and the reaction was instantaneous. Children all over America demanded (and got) the toy; within a few weeks, Mattel could barely keep up. In a few months, Mattel had sold more than a million Burp Guns (Panati, 1991). Mattel successfully redirected the field of children's advertising, moving the emphasis from reaching store buyers and parents to reaching the children directly; this decision was so profitable that other toy companies quickly followed suit.

Sometimes it can be a series of consumers who redirect a field based on a product, rather than the product itself. When the chain of Kmart produced its own bottle of wine ("Kmarto," priced at $1.97), it provided a ripe opportunity for Kmart customers to redirect a purchase of wine into a gag gift. The Kmarto wine was a flop as an actual alcoholic beverage, but several newspapers reported its continued popularity as a joke—one family, for example, was reported to include Kmarto in all of their group photographs (Kirchner, 1996).

Sometimes items succeed because they are not mass-produced (like Kmart wine), but rather are custom-made. Almost any product ordered "custom-made" today will take longer to be produced and will likely be more expensive than off-the-shelf products. For the custom-made price, you are allowed to designate options according to your personal preferences and special needs. Americans living in the nineteenth century enjoyed the luxury (whether they wanted it or not) of custom-made everything, from kitchen cabinets to household machines. But with the introduction of mass production and assembly lines, the standards in industry were about to change, and with them the standard of living of the average American citizen.

Eli Whitney in the United States as well as others in Europe had introduced mass-production techniques to the arms industry. However, a strong promoter of this industrial movement was the assembly line. The first notable assembly line used during the nineteenth century was actually a *disassembly* line. Employees at a Midwest meatpacking company harvested cuts of meat from carcasses hanging from a trolley overhead. When the work at one station was done, the pieces were easily transported to the next point on the line (*History of Work*, 2000).

It was in this context that Henry Ford first launched the constant motion assembly line for the manufacture of the Model T Ford in 1913. Whereas large machines had previously been mass-produced from a single location to which large stocks of components were hauled, Ford's innovation (which actually was proposed by one of his vice presidents) was to install a moving assembly line on which identical parts could be added to the car as it passed down the line (Cardwell, 1994). On the assembly line, a Ford Model T could be produced in 93 minutes. This reduction in time led to a commensurate reduction in cost to the consumer. In particular, this unprecedented cost effectiveness forced Ford's competitors to join him and play the new production game (*History*, 2000).

While his application of this technique to the automobile industry is no great feat of creative thinking, its impact on the field was strongly redirective. Ford's promotion of the assembly line and of mass-production techniques was an impetus with wide-reaching impact. Whereas others had begun using these methods, Ford's introduction of the assembly line and mass production to the assembly of cars initiated a change in manufacturing whose impact reached beyond the automobile industry to include a broad range of industrial domains.

The increased use of mass production has influenced the nature of the industrial workforce, the economies of countries through the world, and has led to related techniques such as automatization. For example, factories rely primarily on unskilled or semiskilled labor while machines have taken over the technical difficulties of the job. As mass-production facilities have become more ambitious, more elaborate supervisory hierarchies have become necessary, and positions for management specialists as well as distributors and salespeople have been created.

Although Ford himself did not conceive of this evolution of manufacturing industry, his introduction of the assembly line and the technique of mass production may be considered the crucial step that led to a complete redirection in the field of manufacturing.

Redirection applies in politics as well as in business. The first several presidents of the United States had established a precedent for what was appropriate behavior upon leaving office. George Washington and John Adams, for example, retired to their families. Thomas Jefferson founded the University of Virginia and devoted his time to that university, while

James Madison edited papers on the Constitution and also helped found the University of Virginia (Eskin, 1998). When John Quincy Adams left the presidency, however, he decided that a former president did not have to leave the arena of politics.

Adams's presidency had generally been considered to be a disappointing one, and Adams was easily defeated by Andrew Jackson when he ran for reelection. But the next year (1830), when he was asked to run for Congress in the Plymouth district, he decided to reenter politics. He won the election and served in the House of Representatives for 17 years until his death. (In fact, Adams died shortly after he suffered a stroke while making a speech in the House of Representatives.) Although not an outstanding president, Adams *was* an outstanding congressman. He was frequently in the center of many congressional debates, and he became especially identified with the antislavery cause, including the Amistad case, which was later turned into a popular movie (Boller, 1991). It was interesting that he not only reentered politics, but reentered at a lower level, a place at which he was more successful.

If Adams had not seen fit to redirect the field of how a president's retirement should be spent, then he would have missed out on a very important part of his political career. He also paved the way for other former presidents who later stayed politically active. While Adams was the only former president to enter Congress, many others stayed in politics. Martin Van Buren, Millard Fillmore, and Theodore Roosevelt all ran for president (in elections held years after they left office); Andrew Johnson served as a senator after he left office; William Howard Taft was the chief justice of the Supreme Court for nine years; Herbert Hoover served as the chairman of several relief organizations during World War II; and Jimmy Carter has remained active as a peace broker and humanitarian (Panati, 1989).

A field can be redirected based on which person is hired for a job. In the summer of 2000, when ABC Sports had to hire a third broadcaster for *Monday Night Football*, they had their pick of nearly anyone. It was a plum position—the other two broadcasters already in place were Al Michaels and Dan Fouts, both outstanding at their jobs and respected in the field. The producer of *Monday Night Football*, Dan Ohlmeyer, decided to move the field in a new direction. Rather than hiring someone who was an expert in football and could speak intelligently about it, Ohlmeyer hired someone who had a competent level of knowledge about football, but also who was an expert at being witty and spontaneous—Dennis Miller, best known for his humorous monologues and shows (and not known at all for his football expertise). As Marc Connolly wrote in his ABC Sports Online column (Connolly, 2001), Ohlmeyer thought like a fan and not like an executive. Rather than basing his decision solely on past policy and what was safe, Ohlmeyer chose a person who he thought would be a fun and smart commentator. This decision began to redirect the field of football commentary into being more of an entertainment production than solely a sports production; the success of such a redirection is yet to be seen.

Redirection can also be seen in the use of eunuchs throughout history. A eunuch is a man whose testes (and, in some cases, entire organ) have been removed. Before the days of the Roman Empire, men were castrated primarily for one of three reasons: to punish a defeated political enemy; to punish a criminal; and in an attempt (usually a misguided one) to alleviate a physical ailment, such as epilepsy. With the Roman Empire, however, came the concept of the eunuch as a sexual toy. Eunuchs who had not had the entire organ removed could still maintain an erection, and rich women prefered having sex with eunuchs because there was no question of an unwanted pregnancy. Wealthy men also preferred having intercourse with eunuchs because of their feminine features (Panati, 1989).

The mutilation of boys for the eventual purpose of making them into sexual toys died out with the Roman Empire, but castration itself did not. In the third century, the Roman church found a new reason to castrate young boys that redirected the field of castrati from providing sexual pleasure to providing musical pleasure. Many church choir pieces at that time had roles for very high tenors. Young children who were physically able to sing the pieces were risks for continued performance both because of their inherent instability and their physical growth. A singer using a falsetto was bound by a limited range. A man who had been castrated when he was a boy, however, still could sing the beautiful and clear notes of a child, with none of the risks that presented themselves by actually using a young boy. The church did not vocally promote castration, but did quietly pay great sums for castrati with beautiful voices (with the usual explanation that the castration was the result of an accidental encounter with a wild boar). When musical styles expanded to include a cappella and opera, many of the castrati with the most beautiful voices became superstars (Panati, 1989).

To summarize, in redirection a contribution moves a field in a new direction. Sometimes, though, the redirection is not actually new, but rather is a variant of an old direction. In this case, one is dealing with a reconstruction/redirection, as discussed in the next chapter.

7
CHAPTER

Reconstruction/Redirection

In using reconstruction/redirection, an individual suggests that the field should move *backward* to a previous point but then should move in a direction divergent from where it has moved. In other words, the individual suggests that at some time in the past, the field went off track. The individual suggests the point at which this occurred and how the field should have moved forward from that point. The work is judged as creative to the extent that the individual is judged as correctly recognizing that the field has gone off track and to the extent that the new direction suggested from the past is viewed as a useful direction for the field to pursue. Of course, sometimes people who use this strategy are simply reintroducing ideas that have been shown to be lacking or simply dead wrong, hoping that their reintroduction of these ideas will somehow make what did not work in the past, work in the present. In such cases, the proposals amount to taking bad wine and trying to sell it in a newer and hopefully classier bottle. Consider examples of reconstruction/redirection in science and technology.

☐ Science and Technology

In the early 1900s, intelligence tests seemed to have potential for helping society understand why certain groups rose to the top of the society and other groups fell to the bottom of that society (see Carroll, 1982; Ceci, 1996; Gould, 1981). This often thinly disguised social Darwinism was based on the notion that those groups with more adaptive skills, on average, should and in fact did tend to have more success in adapting to the demands of the social structure of the society. In contrast, those groups with fewer adaptive skills, on average, did and should fall to the bottom. This kind of thinking became unpopular in the 1960s and 1970s. Environment came to be seen as much more important than it had seemed before (Kamin, 1974; Lewontin, 1982). As a result, intelligence test scores were no longer being looked at as a cause of group differences, but rather, as an effect.

This balance was upset when Herrnstein and Murray (1994) argued that the older views were most likely correct in many respects: It is plausible, they argued, to believe that group differences in IQ are in fact due to genetic factors and that these group differences result in social mobility. Herrnstein and Murray further suggested that what they considered a humane social policy could be constructed on the basis of these alleged facts. Many people who were more comfortable with the older views or who were ready to be persuaded of these views found the Herrnstein–Murray arguments convincing. Others, especially those who believed in multiple intelligences or the importance of environment, were not at all convinced.

Our goal here is not to argue about the validity of the Herrnstein–Murray position, which we have discussed elsewhere (Sternberg, 1995). Rather, it is to suggest that the work of Herrnstein and Murray served a reconstructive function. Herrnstein and Murray suggested that the field had gone off course in the desire of its members to accept certain beliefs that, however charitable they might be, were incorrect. These authors suggested the field return to a point that many (although certainly not all) investigators had thought had been left behind, and that the field then advance from that point.

B. F. Skinner's (1972) analysis of creativity represents another example of a reconstruction/redirection. Skinner apparently was perturbed that the analysis of creativity had moved further and further away from the kinds of behavioristic principles that Skinner and his behavioristic colleagues believed they had shown applied to *all* behavior. The 1972 paper was, in large part, an argument that the field of creativity had lost its foundations, and that it needed to return to the kind of behavioristic analyses that Skinner believed he and others had shown could account for creative behavior.

A further scientific example of a reconstruction/redirection, this one in the biological domain, is Harvey's discovery of the circulation of the blood. William Harvey's (1578–1657) education in anatomy was based on the observations of the Greek scientist, Galen (c. 129–c. 200). Although Galen was viewed as the expert in this field for centuries, sixteenth-century anatomists began to doubt Galen's views based on their own observations. Galen's observance of different-colored blood in the veins and arteries led him to conclude that these were two distinct substances. His theory held that the veins originated in the liver and supplied nourishment to the body. The arteries and heart were regarded as a completely separate system through which the blood provided the body with life-giving air (Meadows, 1987).

However, there were difficulties with Galen's explanations of the functions of the heart and liver. Galen suspected that blood must be able to seep from one side of the heart to the other through the septum wall, but it was difficult to directly see how this system could be possible. Also, Galen's explanation that the blood originated in the liver and became enriched with air through the lungs did not explain why blood appeared in the vein bringing blood *from* the lungs *to* the heart. According to Galen, this order of events is backward. Gradually, skeptics began to find evidence that refuted some of Galen's views. A Paduan professor of anatomy and surgery, Matteo Realdo Colombo (1516–1559), demonstrated that blood passes from one side of the heart to the other, not through the septum directly, but via the lungs (Meadows, 1987).

One point of critique was Galen's disregard for Aristotle's principles of biology. Whereas Aristotelian thought held that the heart was the center of the body and soul, Galen's observations led him to conclude that the liver was a more important organ than the heart, and more controversially, that the brain was the center of thought. In contrast, Harvey remained true to Aristotelian principles, maintaining that the heart was the central organ of the body and soul. In accord with Aristotelian science, Harvey tried to deduce organ functions by observing them directly, criticizing Galen for not founding "his dogmas on experiment or even direct observation" (Cohen, 1985, p. 189). Today it is assumed that scientific knowledge will advance as the result of careful experimentation, but this was not the case in Harvey's day. Harvey's reform of biology can be viewed as the result of a reform on another level, that of methodology. Cohen (1985) points out that "the quantitative method was not then in general use and Harvey was fully aware that his numerical reasoning was as radical in its methods as in its results" (p. 192). Harvey's new methods led him to observe that the valves of the heart allowed blood to flow in one direction only. He also discerned that the great amount of blood present in the body was unlikely to exist in a one-way system. Harvey reasoned that the blood must circulate in a closed system that runs throughout the body. This theory suggested that the arteries carry oxygen-rich blood to the extremities and that the veins transport the blood back toward the heart. This theory was confirmed through simple observations. First, a tight band was positioned on the upper arm, inhibiting blood flow to the hand. As the band was slightly loosened, the arteries were freed and blood rushed into the lower arm and hand. Only when the band was completely removed was blood able to flow into the veins, up and out of the arm, back toward the heart. Both the veins and the arteries were part of a single, closed, circulatory system (Meadows, 1987).

Harvey's discovery of the circulation of the blood was a great leap for biology, making a significant break with historical Galenic anatomy. In this case, the nature of Harvey's creative path was reconstructive. Rather than follow Galen's lead in anatomical investigation, Harvey returned to the Aristotelian ideals of direct observation and hesitated to disregard the heart as an unimportant center of life in the body. In upholding these principles, Harvey redirected his field on two levels. First, his discoveries about biology advanced the field's understanding of the circulatory system. And second, Harvey's research in the Aristotelian tradition demonstrated the value of the empirical method, challenging his field to embark upon a new fork on their methodological path.

Reconstruction/redirection applies in technology as well as in biology. A recent development in amateur photography is the one-use camera. The small unit is purchased preloaded with film, and the film is developed simply by dropping off the camera at a camera center. The film processors remove the film from the camera, develop it, and return the prints to the customer. This convenient service saves consumers the trouble of carrying a fragile, expensive camera with them on vacation. It also gives a second chance to those vacationers who forgot their personal cameras at home. And it even allows newlyweds to collect candid shots of their friends and relatives at their wedding reception without having to hire a professional. Do you think this is a wonderful example of an invention for modern convenience? Think again.

Actually, the one-use camera was invented in 1888, one of the original Kodaks to be marketed to amateurs (Flatow, 1992). The first cameras for personal use were marketed under the motto, "You press the button, we do the rest," a slogan that would certainly apply to many of today's automatic cameras (Flatow, 1992, p. 49). Whereas early photography was characterized by its reliance on cumbersome equipment and dangerous chemicals, this new Kodak was improved for amateur use. Kodak's first personal camera was small and lightweight. Its film was stored in a compact roll that could be unwound with a key. And the operation of the camera required no special chemicals or setup. Consumers bought a camera that was preloaded with a roll of film of 100 exposures. When the roll was shot, the entire camera was shipped to Kodak for processing and returned fully reloaded and ready to go.

By 1900, Eastman Kodak had perfected his concept of the personal-use camera with the introduction of the Brownie camera. The six-exposure

Brownie was cheap, extremely simple to use, and caught the imaginations of many Americans (Flatow, 1992).

The reinvention of the original Kodak as a modern one-use, disposable camera is an example of a creative reconstruction/redirection. The Kodak company recognized the potential of this old idea to move the field in a new direction. Whereas the original camera first enabled nonprofessionals to try their hand at photography, the modern reconstruction contributes in a different way. In the field of modern photography, it is no new concept that amateurs have access to quality cameras, so the creative contribution of the new Kodak original is its convenience. Now there is an option for people who seek an inexpensive, temporary solution to their photography needs. Wouldn't they be surprised to learn that a similar convenience existed at the turn of the century?

☐ Arts and Letters

Examples of reconstruction/redirection can be found in the arts and letters as well as in science and technology. Some literary scholars are now suggesting that literary criticism has gone off track—that the kind of deconstructionism introduced by Derrida (1992) and others—where virtually "anything goes" in terms of literary interpretation—has produced a literary nihilism that has resulted in a degeneration of the field of literary criticism. These individuals, such as Bloom (1994), suggest that literary scholars return to their earlier tradition of finding meaning in literary works rather than asserting that virtually any meaning can be read into any literary work.

In the world of painting, Joan Mitchell can be seen as an example of an artistic reconstructor/redirector. Her works (especially those painted in the 1980s) reflect the colors and themes of Monet's landscape paintings. She uses Monet as a base from which to expand, rather than incorporating more recent styles (Hartt, 1993). Indeed, she spent much of her later life in France, where the impressionist style of Monet and other artists was created.

Recent "sequels" to classic works of literature are further examples of reconstruction/redirection. Not merely trying to re-create past works, these "sequels" attempt to both advance the plot and apply modern sensibilities to the novels. In Alexandra Ripley's *Scarlett*, the titular heroine of *Gone with the Wind* becomes less needy and less man dependent, reflecting a society's changing values. Laura Kalpakian's *Cosette* follows the surviving characters from *Les Miserables* and allows readers to see how Marius and Cosette would have handled the upcoming French Revolution.

This is not to say that reconstructive and redirectors cannot create their own unique ideas. A neoclassicist of the early twentieth century, German composer Paul Hindemith believed in the importance of order, stability, and continuity with tradition. Whereas composers of the romantic era challenged the bounds of tonality with their roaming harmonies and Schoenberg went so far as to propose a new musical language in which all 12 tones were equal, Hindemith explained how those 12 tones were necessarily located around a tonal center. Hindemith revived the use of absolute forms characteristic of the classical era. This effort addressed his concern for the audience's ability to understand music. Hindemith warned that straying too far from prototypical structure, melody, and harmony would render much of the art inaccessible to its lay listeners.

An example of the artist's attitude toward musical composition is his symphony *Mathis der Maler* (1934). This work re-creates classical sonata form with a twentieth-century tonal twist. Rather than moving from tonic to dominant throughout a movement, Hindemith's tonic tends to pull toward the tritone. Although this progression is far from traditional, the recurring tritone actually unifies the work, leading Kemp (1980) to call it a "coherently argued whole" (p. 582). Kemp also praises the composer for his synthesis of old and new: "Hindemith developed a language that restores the validity of tonality as a structural and expressive tool, while at the same time remaining unmistakably original in its absorption of both traditional and twentieth-century harmonic resources" (p. 582). Hindemith hinted at the past not only in his use of tonality and traditional form, but also the programmatic elements found in *Mathis* hearken back to the romantic contributions of the nineteenth century. Not only Hindemith, but also such neoclassicists as Stravinsky, Milhaud, and Poulenc, affirmed the relevance of absolute forms, counterpoint, and tonality in their musical compositions of the early twentieth century (Machlis, 1979).

☐ Popular Culture

Reconstruction/redirection can be found in the popular culture as well as in the more classical arts and letters. The musical *Take It Easy* (1996) is an exemplar of reconstruction/redirection. Author Raymond G. Fox's musical takes place in the 1940s, and the music is a reconstruction of the "swing" sound. The characters are intentionally stereotypes, such as The Bookworm and The All-American Hero. The ultimate goal of the show is to re-create the feel of a 1940s college musical, with young, good-looking, and patriotic characters. Several other recent Broadway shows, such as *Triumph of Love* (book by James Magruder, music by Jeffrey Stock, and lyrics by Susan Birkenhead) and *Big* (book by John Weidman, music by

David Shire, and lyrics by Richard Maltby, Jr.) have been "throwback" musicals that reflect the more simplistic plot, characters, and musical tone of musicals of the 1950s. Unlike more modern shows, which tend to be entirely sung and have either an operatic or rock musical style, these shows take the structure and values of more classic musicals (such as *Oklahoma!* or *My Fair Lady*) and update the topics and sensibilities to the 1990s (e.g., in *Big*, characters refer to rap music).

Consider reconstruction/redirection as it applies to politics. Many very conservative politicians, who hark back to a better and simpler age, exemplify the reconstruction/redirection kind of propulsion. These politicians believe that politics—indeed, perhaps, the entire world—would be better served by undoing the last several decades of domestic and foreign policy and starting from scratch. One politician who exemplifies this viewpoint—and who has written and spoken extensively on how he would have handled crises and situations of the past—is Pat Buchanan. In an age when people often watch what they say and are careful not to offend potential voters, Buchanan nonetheless has spoken his mind.

Buchanan has criticized immigration, believing that America's demographic population should stay constant. He strongly believes in American isolationism and goes so far as to criticize America's entrance into World War II. If he had been president, Buchanan states, he would have left Hitler alone; Nazi Germany's objectives did not directly affect the United States (Cohen, 1999).

Buchanan, while often being extreme to the point of seriously offending people, is still a politician in search of a perhaps reactionary constituency. Other groups who have also reconstructed and redirected a field have had much more sinister motivations. Holocaust deniers, or "revisionists," have claimed either that the Holocaust (in which the Nazis killed more than 10 million people who were deemed undesirable) never occurred, or else that the Holocaust has been greatly exaggerated. This tactic can be examined in depth by looking at the various attacks on the veracity of *The Diary of Anne Frank* (Frank, 1952).

As many people know, Anne Frank was a young Jewish schoolgirl who went into hiding with her family and other acquaintances for 25 months. Her family was then discovered by the Nazis, and everyone but her father was killed. A group of Holocaust deniers, however, claim that Anne Frank never existed.

They begin by reconstructing the past. Meyer Levin was a writer who was one of the first people to review *The Diary of Anne Frank*, and he was later hired by Anne's father, Otto Frank, to adapt the diary into a stage play. Levin and Otto Frank disagreed about the nature of such a play— Frank wanted to make the story more universal, while Levin wanted to keep the story firmly rooted in the young girl's Judaism (Graver, 1995).

When Frank hired other writers to adapt the diary (Albert Hackett and Francis Goodrich, who won the Pulitzer Prize for the play), Levin filed a lawsuit for damages, claiming, in part, that some of the completed play by Hackett and Goodrich was, in fact, based on his version of the play.

This lawsuit, which was eventually settled out of court, provided fodder for the revisionists to reconstruct the past. Despite much evidence to the contrary (including the seemingly incontrovertible presence, as tracked down by Simon Wiesenthal [1967], of the Nazi who admitted responsibility for capturing her), attacks on the truth of the diary began by the 1960s. Writers such as Teressa Hendry have made the suggestion that Levin wrote the diary, and by 1975, David Irving claimed (incorrectly) that this suggestion had been "proven" (Lipstadt, 1993). In 1978, Ditlieb Felderer published a sexually explicit book that put forth the argument that not only is the diary a hoax, but also that it is child pornography. Throughout the late 1970s, several individuals, many of them neo-Nazis, distributed pamphlets throughout West Germany, which also claimed that the diary was a hoax.

It was not until several events occurred in rapid succession in the late 1970s and early 1980s that these accusations were mostly muted. Otto Frank sued several of the pamphleteers in court and won; David Irving was continually ruled against in the courtroom; and, upon Frank's death, the Netherlands State Institute for War Documentation conducted a long series of tests on the diaries. These tests ranged from handwriting analysis to examining the glue in the binding and the ink of the page. All of the results were consistent with Anne Frank—and only Anne Frank—having written her diary (Lipstadt, 1993).

The revisionists—at least in the case of *The Diary of Anne Frank*—met with stiff resistance. But examining their goals stripped of ethical implications reveals a desire to reconstruct the field of history, and redirect it in another manner. Creative or propulsive acts are not always conducted in the best interests of humankind.

Reconstruction/redirection need not be of such a serious nature. The mah-jongg craze of the 1920s represents a very American fad, and also a reconstruction/redirection. Mah-jongg was a game for wealthy Chinese men for many years (although not by that name); played with exotic tiles, the game is a mix of dice and dominoes (Panati, 1991). An American named Joseph Babcock observed the popularity of the nineteenth-century game in China, especially as a high-stakes form of gambling. Babcock brought the game with him to America, created his own sets, and began selling them; the craze began in California and soon spread to the rest of America. With mah-jongg came an interest in many objects from traditional China, such as fans, kimonos, and teas. Babcock and the subsequent game developers and marketers took the field of leisure and game playing and looked backward for inspiration, yet they then redirected the nature of the game to be more commercial. The vast sums of money often gambled by Asian men were replaced by small bets, mostly among American housewives (Panati, 1991). While mah-jongg is still played today, its immense popularity soon died out (in part because cheaper copies of the game flooded the market, making it less exclusive).

A modest Broadway hit of the mid-1980s represents another example of the reconstruction/redirection kind of propulsion. Rupert Holmes (a singer/songwriter perhaps best known at that time for the "Pina Colada song") became drawn to Charles Dickens's last novel, *The Mystery of Edwin Drood*. The story of Edwin Drood was a typical Dickensian tale of romantic love, innocent heroines, murky villains, and coincidences. Young Drood has been betrothed to sweet Rosa Bud for many years, but their feelings for each other were closer to sister and brother. Drood's uncle, Jasper, is also Rosa's music teacher and has impure thoughts about the girl. Visiting twins from Ceylon, Neville and Helena Landress, add exotic mystery to the mix, as does the kindly Reverend Crisparkle and Princess Puffer, who runs the local opium den. When Drood disappears, leaving behind only a bloodstained coat, there are plenty of suspects.

Unfortunately for mystery buffs, however, Dickens died before completing the novel. Drood's true killer will remain unknown. But Holmes wanted to turn the story into a musical, and he did not let the lack of an ending stop him. The first thing he did was to perfectly capture the era in which Dickens wrote *The Mystery of Edwin Drood*. The show was set in an English musical hall, and performed by a local troupe of players. The host for the evening was the lively chairman of the troupe, and he introduced each character and identified which member of the troupe was playing the role. As was popular at that time, young Edwin Drood was played by a woman.

After reconstructing an evening of entertainment from Dickensian times, Holmes then proceeded to tell the story in a conventional manner of that day, until the point at which Dickens died. When this part of the story occurred, the show was stopped. The chairman appealed to the audience for help, and the actors were sent out into the audience with notepads and pens. The audience then voted on the killer (as well as the true identity of a mysterious detective). The actors tallied up the votes, and the show then was performed based on the choices of the audience. Holmes wrote many different endings, so there are 30 different possibilities that can be performed (before, in a nice twist, Drood is revealed to be alive, having survived his attack). *The Mystery of Edwin Drood* uses old source material and an old method of storytelling, but then moves the concept in a new direction.

Reconstruction/redirection can apply in politics. Much of the political philosophy of Thomas Jefferson is rooted in reconstruction/redirection. Jefferson was fascinated with the life and writings of Solon, an Athenian statesman and politician who lived from 638 to 559 B.C. Solon was an early exponent of the concept of city-and-state republican democracy. He was a moderate reformer who experimented a great deal in early forms of republican government. Many of his ideas about the nature of citizenship, with a person's privileges commersurate with their responsibilities, were a basis for Jefferson's political ideas and beliefs.

However, rather than merely harking back to an ancient Greek model, Jefferson also incorporated more modern ideas about government (such as those of Thomas Hobbes and Adam Smith), and his eventual philosophy was, perhaps, what Solon's philosophies would have been if the Greek politician had enjoyed the benefit of another two thousand years of discoveries and ideas (Ellis, 1998). Jefferson's political philosophy was certainly put to great use in his lifetime as a politician and writer; in addition to writing the Declaration of Independence, Jefferson served as minister to France, secretary of state, vice president, and president, and he helped found the democratic–republican party, which succeeded the federalist party to become the predominant political party in America for many years (Ferris, 1973).

In sum, reconstruction/redirection involves taking ideas in a direction that is new with respect to the present but, oddly enough, not with respect to the past. However, as in redirection, one maintains the starting point of the existing paradigm. In another kind of creativity, reinitiation, discussed in the next chapter, one not only moves in a new direction, but also fixes on a new starting point to begin one's work.

8

CHAPTER

Reinitiation

Reinitiation is a form of paradigm-rejecting contribution that restarts the field in a new place and moves in a new direction from there. In reinitiation, a contributor suggests that a field or subfield has reached an undesirable point or has exhausted itself moving in its current direction. But rather than suggesting that the field or subfield change course (as in redirection), the contributor suggests moving in a different direction from a different point in the multidimensional space of contributions. In effect, the contributor is suggesting people question their assumptions and "start over" from a point that most likely makes different assumptions. This form of creative contribution represents a major paradigm shift and comes closest to Kuhn's (1970) conception of revolutionary science. Martindale (1990) has pointed out that here what we call reinitiations also occur in the arts. And at least some of the innovators in Kirton's theory of adaptors and innovators (e.g., Kirton, Bailey, & Glendinning, 1991) would fall into this category as well. Consider examples of reinitiation from the domains of science and technology.

☐ Science and Technology

Two notable examples of this kind of creativity can be found in the contributions to intelligence made by Spearman (1904) and by Binet and Simon (1916). Spearman reinvented intelligence theory and research when he created factor analysis and proposed the two-factor theory (general ability and also specific abilities of lesser interest), based on his factor-analytic results. Spearman's contribution was to put theorizing about intelligence on a firm quantitative footing, a contribution that lives on today, whether or not one agrees with either Spearman's theory or his methodology. Binet and Simon (1905/1916) reinvented intelligence measurement. Whereas Galton (1883) had proposed that intelligence should be understood in terms of simple psychophysical processes, Binet and Simon suggested that it should be understood instead in terms of higher-order processes of judgment. For the most part, the measurements of intelligence today are still based on this notion of Binet and Simon.

Spearman's (1904, 1927) reinitiating emphasis on general ability was not shared by all investigators. For example, Thurstone (1938), Guilford (1967), and many other theorists suggested that intelligence comprises multiple abilities and that any general factor obtained in factor analyses was likely to be at best unimportant, and at worst epiphenomenal. In all cases, however, intelligence was accepted as a unitary construct: What differed were investigators' views on how, if at all, the unitary construct should be divided.

Festinger and Carlsmith's (1959) initial paper on cognitive dissonance, mentioned earlier, represents a reinitiation, an attempt to make a new start in social psychology. A more recent example of a reinitiation is Bem's (1996) theory of homosexuality, which is that what an individual initially finds exotic later in life becomes erotic. Bem's theory argues for environmental causes of homosexuality at a time when biological theories largely have gained acceptance.

Revolutionary works tend to be major reinitiations. In linguistics, for example, Chomsky's (1957) transformational grammar changed the way many linguists viewed language. Linguists following Chomsky began analyzing deep syntactic structures, not just surface structures.

One example of a theory that completely upset a prevailing theory of its day was Copernicus's proposal of a heliocentric universe. In the early sixteenth century, the predominant view of the nature of the universe was a geocentric one. Natural philosophers had observed the moon's revolution about the Earth and had concluded that distant planets and stars, including the sun, were part of this geocentric universe. One proponent of this view was Ptolemy, who described the motion of heavenly bodies in equants—noncircular, nonuniform orbits around the Earth. Copernicus disagreed with this model for a reason based on principle: He believed that the planets must travel in uniform, circular orbits (Cohen, 1985).

Not only did Copernicus distrust the Ptolemaic postulate regarding the nature of orbits, but he also dared to question a fundamental assumption of planetary motion: Copernicus could not accept that the Earth was the center of the universe. Copernicus's model held that there was a static center to the universe. According to his calculations, it was more sensible to allow the Earth to rotate around this static center along with the rest of the planets. It was Johannes Kepler who took the next step and put the sun in this central position, making the Copernican model explicitly heliocentric. Ironically, Copernicus's scientific ideal regarding the motion of the planets was later disproved with the discovery of elliptical orbits. The major contribution of Copernican astronomy has always been hailed as its "radical break" with Ptolemaic astronomy, which pushed the Earth aside and put the sun in its rightful position as the center of the solar system (Cohen, 1985).

Cohen (1985) has argued that the Copernican revolution was no revolution at all, given that it had little influence on the field at the time. In fact, Copernicus anticipated that his ideas would be met with distrust and, for these reasons, he hesitated to publish his treatise until 1543, just before his death. It was only after the telescope became available that Galileo was able to validate Copernicus's theory. Galileo observed that the Earth was not the only planet to have a moon. With the loss of this key piece of evidence in favor of the geocentric view, combined with further observations of the sky, Galileo was convinced that planets orbited by moons may still themselves be in orbit around a separate central body, namely, the sun (Meadows, 1987).

Kepler's revision of the Copernican model followed by Galileo's observational confirmations brought attention to the Copernican model, causing the effects of Copernicus's revolutionary ideas to be felt across the scientific world. The acceptance of the new model of the universe was indeed a reinitiation, a step that rejected the previous model and built a new one. While Kepler and Galileo's contributions refined and improved upon the Copernican model in an incremental way, the initial proposal of Copernicus was the reinitiative contribution that produced the discontinuity necessary for others to make headway in our understanding of the organization of the universe.

Another reinitiation in science was Lavoisier's revolutionary new chemistry. In contrast to the Copernican revolution, this reinitiation had an immediate and lasting impact on the field. In the eighteenth century, the predominant view of combustion was that of the German chemist Georg Stahl (1660–1734). Stahl's model of combustion was founded on the premise that combustible matter was composed of water and a substance called phlogiston. According to this early view, burning a metal resulted in the loss of phlogiston. Support for this theory was demonstrated by combining the oxide of a metal with a material containing phlogiston (for example, charcoal). This experiment would yield a pure sample of the metal, consistent with the theory that the addition of phlogiston could restore the initial substance (Meadows, 1987).

However, it became clear that chemical reactions of combustion yielded slightly heavier products, despite the claim that the process of combustion required the loss of matter, namely, phlogiston. This apparent paradox led many chemists of the day to attempt to explain the result in the context of phlogiston theory. However, Antoine Lavoisier (1743–1794) was skeptical enough of the vague and sparse evidence for the actual existence of this mysterious substance called phlogiston that he dared to discard the concept altogether. Lavoisier proceeded to explain how combustion could take place in its absence. Based on careful analysis, Lavoisier confirmed through observation that metals actually did gain weight during combustion. This result was attributed to the presence of oxygen during combustion. When a metal burned, oxygen in the air was consumed and was captured in the resulting compound, an oxide (Cohen, 1985).

The key failure of phlogiston theory is its lack of an understanding of the gaseous state. Early chemists did not consider air to play a role in combustion reactions. At most, the air was a mere waste bin for the phlogiston lost in the reaction. Lavoisier discovered that elements could exist in solid, liquid, and gaseous states. It was this realization that became the foundation of Lavoisier's chemical revolution. Lavoisier pointed out that air is composed of many different substances, one of which is oxygen.

In contrast to the Copernican delayed revolution, Lavoisier's revolution in chemistry made an impact almost immediately. Through the introduction of a standardized chemical language, a new periodical in 1788, a textbook in 1789, and a host of disciples, the new chemistry became respected by all but a few skeptical scientists (notably, Joseph Priestly) within a few decades (Meadows, 1987). This revolution is known as the triumph of the Antiphlogistians (Cohen, 1985).

Lavoisier's opposition to phlogiston theory was not a radical leap from the normal science of his time. Phlogiston theory was not well supported by the available data. However, Lavoisier's confident declaration of his rejection of this long-held theory and his suggestion of a plausible alternative view reinitiated chemistry. Especially notable are Lavoisier's subsequent contributions to the field in terms of developing a standardized chemical language and his laying out a textbook describing the new chemistry (Meadows, 1987). In this way, the contribution of a new chemical theory was not merely a next logical step, but a reinitiation from a new starting point that rejected what had been crucial assumptions of the field.

A revolution took place in medicine in the nineteenth century as a result of Pasteur's proposal of the germ theory of disease. Before Pasteur, disease was believed to be transmitted through odors. The miasmatic theory held that diseases were caused from tiny particles in fumes (miasma) exuding from decaying dumps of natural waste. Early theories about the causes of disease also included belief in the principle of spontaneous generation, or the principle that something can come from nothing. One proponent of this view was French scientist Felix-Archimede Pouchet, who proposed that the growth of maggots on corpses was a result of the spontaneous generation of life from nonlife. Pouchet claimed that only air and water needed to combine with decaying matter in order for organisms to grow; a biological explanation was not necessary (Meadows, 1987).

However, Pasteur's experience with fermentation and bacterial cultures suggested to him that decay was similar to fermentation, and therefore living microorganisms (bacteria) were necessary for decay to occur. In response to Pouchet's claims, Pasteur designed an experiment to demonstrate that air alone was not sufficient to cause decay. His idea was to put a solution in a flask with a swanlike neck. Such a flask had free access to air, but did not permit bacteria to reach the solution. When no life developed in the flasks, Pouchet had to admit that air itself was not responsible for generation of life, and that Pasteur's bacterial hypothesis was correct (Meadows, 1987).

This success was a crucial step in Pasteur's path toward the germ theory of disease. If bacteria were present in air, then these microbes could be responsible for the contagion of disease. This new theory would necessarily overthrow the old miasmatic one, replacing it with a biological explanation for the origin of disease, a medical reinitiation.

In fact, Pasteur's new hypothesis already had preliminary supportive evidence based on experiences in the medical field. Over the years, scientists and medical professionals had made observations about the nature of bacterial diseases. Even before bacteria had been discovered, John Snow (1813–1858) noticed in 1854 that cholera was spread through water. Ignaz Semmelweis (1818–1865) realized that simple practices such as washing hands and instruments between patients could curb the contagion of puerperal fever among children attended to by the same interns and nurses. Heat had also been observed to deter contagion for certain diseases.

Whereas medical professionals had learned through observation some major principles of the germ theory of disease, Pasteur's theory provided a mechanism for these effects and legitimated the intuitions of these doctors' careful observations. Pasteur's proposal that it was bacteria in air that were passed between patients through unwashed hands and unheated instruments proved that odors in air could not be responsible for infection but rather that a new assumption, that microbes were present in air, could account for the contagion of disease. This revolution in medicine created a new starting point for the study of infectious diseases and led to a variety of medical discoveries, including vaccine therapy and the practice of antisepsis in surgery.

☐ Arts and Letters

Reinitiations occur in the arts and letters as well as in science and technology. Reinitiative contributions are often bold and daring gestures. One prime example can be found in sculpture, with Marcel Duchamp's 1917 *Fountain*. Duchamp's Dada piece is simply a urinal turned on its back. The very act of entering such a piece in an art show is a statement about art—Duchamp's sculpture made artists focus on the definition of exactly what art is and what art can be. Duchamp's urinal became a piece of art, and he and his fellow Dada creators set the stage for other modern art that exists, in part, to challenge our ideas of what "art" encompasses (Hartt, 1993).

Another radical reinitiator is one of Duchamp's friends, the composer John Cage, who often employed unconventional sound materials. During one period, his compositional process (and often performance) was determined entirely by chance. The philosophy that led Cage to compose in this unorthodox manner can be considered essentially a rejection of some basic tenets of the Western musical tradition, including the definition of music itself. Cage declared music to be all sound, including the whispers and heartbeats we perceive while silent. Cage's affinity for Eastern philosophy caused him to focus on the importance of awareness in the human experience, and he used his music to foster awareness in his listeners.

An illustration of this point is his piece *4' 33."* The performance of this piece consists of four minutes and 33 seconds of "silence," or rather, in Cage's terminology, "unintentional sound." In performance, the instrumentalist approaches her instrument, prepares to play, and proceeds to sit, motionless and without sound, for four minutes and 33 seconds. The only pauses are those indicated by Cage that signal the change of movement. The music, therefore, is the sound that exists in the environment during that period of time. Cage's statement is that there is music being played around us constantly; we must expand the notion of music as organized melody, harmony, and rhythm to include all intentional sound, even the rush of traffic beyond the door and the buzzing of the fluorescent lights above our heads (Cage, 1961; Hamm, 1980).

Dancer and choreographer Paul Taylor is a similar reinitiator. He performed a solo piece reminiscent of Cage's work in which he merely stood still for four minutes while on stage. What is notable about this performance is that the journalist who was assigned to review the dance for *Dance Observer* wrote an equally radical review: four inches of blank white space! (Fadiman, 1985).

Reinitiations in literature are plentiful. Some famous examples are James Joyce's *Finnegan's Wake* (written in stream of consciousness) and many of Franz Kafka's stories (such as *Metamorphosis*, the story of a man who wakes up and discovers he has turned into a cockroach). William Burroughs, best known for *Naked Lunch* (1959), broke new ground with his use of vulgarity, graphic scatology, and obscene language. Paranoid and sadistic, his best work brilliantly explores issues of control and freedom, often using the metaphor of drug use. Much of his work also often explores (in very different ways) his accidental slaying of his wife (Parker & Kermode, 1996). Ian Finlay's poetry transcends nearly any type of poetry done before, with its use of such visual props as wild flowers, stone, sundials, and glass combining with the words of the poetry to result in the overall creation of a certain emotion or feeling (Parker & Kermode, 1996).

☐ Popular Culture

Reinitiations can totally change the popular culture. An unlikely example of reinitiation can be found in the work of Jesus Christ. If we set aside religious issues and look at his leadership abilities—as Jay Haley did in his popular essay *The Power Tactics of Jesus Christ* (1969)—we find a brilliant revolutionary who used unheard-of tactics and completely innovative strategies. When Jesus first began his work, the field of leadership was in some ways very similar to and in other ways very different from what it is today. The leaders of that time were almost all Roman and wealthy. Jesus was neither. Other revolutionaries who attempted to use religion as a method of organizing the people invariably criticized the current system and called for the development of a new religion, and these same revolutionaries were then quickly marked for death by the Romans or the high priests.

What Jesus did was completely different. He said that he did not call for a revision of the law or the current religious practices, yet he then preached for a complete revision of these same laws and religious practices. Jesus said that he was not rewriting or changing the religious laws, but rather interpreting them in a different way. Jesus never made any blatantly anti-Roman statements that could be later used against him. And while other leaders would spread the word of their powers and gifts, Jesus would tell those people whom he healed to keep it a secret. As Haley (1969) says, few people who have been suddenly cured of a serious illness will, in fact, keep such a secret, yet if the Romans or high priests confronted Jesus on his healing abilities, he could honestly say that he had never claimed he had such powers.

Jesus also was a reinitiator in terms of collecting his following. Rather than working in the established power system, Jesus took the opposite route, and gathered his people from the poverty-stricken and powerless. His teachings, indeed, argue that it is the poor who will enter heaven first, and Jesus himself lived as a poor man. Jesus developed an enormous following among the poor, and this following has lasted well beyond his death—indeed, to the present day. Most leaders of any significant revolutionary movement have used very similar tactics as those pioneered by Jesus (Haley, 1969).

While a reinitiation can certainly be the result of a great leader like Jesus, or of a great writer like James Joyce, unemployed advertising men can have reinitiative ideas as well, if on a different scale. In 1975, Gary Dahl listened to his friends talk about how expensive and time consuming it was to own a pet. Dogs and cats are not a simple responsibility, and even lower-maintenance pets like fish or birds require a lot of time, effort, and money. It was at this point that Dahl had the idea that a pet did not have to be a living creature. And, in fact, he proceeded along in that direction to create an entirely new idea: a pet rock (Panati, 1991).

While primarily (of course) a parody of pet owners, the pet rock does represent an entirely new way of looking at what it means to own a pet. Dahl took the idea and expanded on it. He wrote an owner's manual (which included instructions on how to train the pet rock to roll over or play dead). He packaged it in a box with air holes, and he also sold pet food, in the form of rock salt (Panati, 1991). The pet rock, as many people know, became an instant success; it is one of the few fads that is still remembered years later. Dahl may not have been intending to make a creative statement, but he did. He conceptualized the field of pet ownership as being in a different place, and then he showed a new place for that field to go. And, indeed, perhaps the current feelings of possessiveness and ownership that some people feel for their personal computers is not that far removed from the odd tenderness one might feel for a pet rock.

Reinitiations can occur in politics as well. Eleanor Roosevelt's term as First Lady represented a reinitiation from what it previously had meant to serve in this capacity. Prior First Ladies had remained in the background and had, for the most part, let their husbands and their husbands' advisors determine their actions. Eleanor Roosevelt was very much her own person, and she approached being the First Lady in an entirely different manner than anyone before her. Her new style became evident only a few days after her husband Franklin was elected president. The outgoing First Lady, Lou Hoover, invited her to the executive mansion. When Hoover asked when the White House limousine should arrive at Roosevelt's hotel, Eleanor said that she would walk. Overcoming the chief of protocol's objections over this simple act, she walked from her hotel to the White House (and walked back, too). This incident was a small indicator of things to come (Boller, 1988).

From the small details to the larger issue of her role in society, Eleanor Roosevelt took charge of her life and behavior in a way that no First Lady had ever done. She ran the White House elevator herself. She helped her servants arrange the furniture when she moved in. She held her own press conferences (something that was unheard of at the time). One reason for Roosevelt's independence, incidentally, was accidental. In 1918, she discovered that her husband was having an affair. While Eleanor and Franklin reached a reconciliation, their marriage was never quite as close. As a result, Eleanor was determined even more to be her own person (Boller, 1988).

Eleanor Roosevelt not only changed the conception of what a First Lady could be, she also took steps to demonstrate the many positive things that a First Lady could accomplish. She personally inspected the slums of Washington, coal mines, and mental hospitals (among many others), and then kept the press informed of what she found. She made tremendous strides for civil rights and women's rights. When she discovered that the Daughters of the American Revolution had refused to give permission to African American singer Marian Anderson to sing in Constitution Hall, Roosevelt resigned from the group and then sponsored an outdoor concert for Anderson at the Lincoln Memorial. She wrote monthly columns for magazines, daily columns for newspapers, and an autobiography, and then donated her earnings from her writing to charity (Boller, 1988). While other First Ladies had certainly helped charity or supported causes passively, Eleanor Roosevelt was the first one to aggressively and actively pursue activities that were important to her. First Ladies such as Jackie Kennedy, Betty Ford, and Hilary Clinton were able to establish their own identities in ways that would have been unimagined before Eleanor Roosevelt pioneered the course.

Around the same time that Eleanor Roosevelt was serving as a reinitiator, another pioneer was serving to reinitiate the role of women in society— only this pioneer was a partly fictional composite, Rosie the Riveter. Before World War II, the idea of women entering the workforce en masse may have seemed far-fetched. But with many of the able-bodied men off fighting in Europe, factories lost workers at the exact time that factory products (such as weapons and airplanes) were most needed. Factories and officials (at such plants as Douglas Aircraft in Long Beach, California) changed the public's perception of working women, shifting the image from an undesirable one to a highly desirable one (Frank, Ziebarth, & Field, 1982).

This change was enacted, in part, through songs, paintings, and posters. The 1942 song "Rosie the Riveter" made the idea of a woman working in a factory seem to be both patriotic and important. Norman Rockwell and other well-known artists created images of Rosie the Riveter; these pictures were then used in posters and flyers. A real-life "Rosie" was soon found in the person of a factory riveter named Rose Monroe, who was then used in many propaganda films (Honey, 1984). The character of Rosie the Riveter inspired women around America, and not only toward factory work. More than six million women joined the various branches of the military to work in a variety of capacities. Many women were not paid; those who were, however, were paid significantly less than men—skilled female workers made much less money than unskilled male workers. When the war ended, the government launched another campaign to get "Rosie" back to the kitchen and away from the factory so that the soldiers returning from the war could have their jobs back. This campaign, however, was much less successful—the original Rosie the Riveter drive inadvertently spurred on the women's movement (Frank, Ziebarth, & Field, 1982). Sometimes reinitiations can push the field in ways that the original creators may not initially have envisioned.

Reinitiations can occur in the everyday use of language. Imagine you were raised to communicate in a language that was only spoken and that had no written form. Suppose you wanted to create a system to represent the sounds and meanings of your native tongue. Where would you start? How many symbols would you need to sufficiently record the multitude of nuances in your oral tradition?

This is exactly the challenge that Cherokee Native American Sequoyah took upon himself in 1809. Sequoyah grew up in Alabama and fought the White settlers in the early 1800s. In 1809, when Sequoyah was approximately 35 years old, he realized that the Cherokee language might suffer under the effects of the social upheaval taking place at the time, so he decided he would do what he could to preserve the oral tradition with which he and his people had been raised. Unfamiliar with any particular written language, English or otherwise, Sequoyah began to create symbols to represent the sounds of Cherokee.

As he noted the many sounds that were part of his spoken words, he took symbols found in printed materials, including some from the English, Greek, and Arabic alphabets to represent these sounds. In 1821, after 12 years of hard work, Sequoyah had created a list of 85 syllables, the Cherokee syllabary. Based on this syllabary, Sequoyah began to read and write and to teach others to do the same. By 1828, the *Cherokee Phoenix* became the first Native American newspaper. The fact that this written language was created single-handedly and so quickly, is a feat of genius and perseverance (Zahoor, 1999).

The contribution of Sequoyah to the written language may be viewed as a reinitiation through the alphabets he employed in creating it. Sequoyah took letters from English, Greek, and Arabic and assigned to them entirely new Cherokee phonemes, without any regard to their sounds in the original languages. Although there is no reason to believe that Sequoyah did this with the intent to reject the source alphabets, his new syllabary is effectively a reinitiation of the alphabets he drew on in creating his Cherokee syllabary.

So, reinitiations represent new starting points and new directions. An eighth type of contribution is different from all those that have been considered up to now in that it represents neither an acceptance of a particular old paradigm nor the proposal of a new paradigm. Rather, it represents an integration of paradigms, either old with old or old with new. Last, we consider in the next chapter this eighth kind of creativity, integration.

9
CHAPTER

Integration

In this kind of creative contribution, the creator unites two (or more) types of ideas that previously were seen as unrelated or even as opposed. What formerly were viewed as distinct ideas now are viewed as related and capable of being unified. Integration is a key means by which progress is attained in the sciences. (See Thagard [1992] for an extensive discussion of the nature of integration in the sciences.) Consider examples of integrations in science and technology.

☐ Science and Technology

Isaac Newton (1642–1727) is well known for his formulation of the universal law of gravity. In essence, this discovery was a synthesis of ideas proposed by thinkers such as Ptolemy, Copernicus, Kepler, Galileo, and Hooke. Newton succeeded in explaining how a singular concept of gravity could explain a variety of observations made by scientists past and contemporary. While Copernicus had dared to oppose the Ptolemaic notion that planets encircle the sun and Kepler had demonstrated that the orbits were elliptical, no one had been able to explain why such elliptical orbits would emerge. Newton discerned the mathematical rule by which elliptical orbits would result, thus explaining the relationship between planets and the sun. In his 1687 "The Mathematical Principles of Natural Philosophy," Newton described basic principles that could mathematically account for the diverse predictions made by Copernicus and Kepler.

This contribution is a grand synthesis. Not only did Newton bring together a variety of ideas to explain planetary motion, he also recognized the relationship of this phenomenon to another and essentially integrated the two problems by offering a single solution to both. Newton showed that his principles governing the movement of bodies in the sky could also account for a second, formerly unrelated, problem: that of the motion of objects on the Earth. Essentially, Newton's universal law of gravity declared that matter attracts matter. That is, the sun attracts the planets just as the Earth's gravity pulls on objects near its surface. By achieving this insight, Newton explained two major physical questions of his time with one universal law, an integrative contribution that has remained the basis of physics ever since.

Consider an example of integration as it applies in the biological sciences. Charles Darwin (1809–1882) was not the originator of the concept of evolution. However, he is famous because his theory successfully synthesized the leading theories of his day into a convincing explanation for the evolution of species.

One of the best-known proponents of an evolutionary biological history was Jean Baptiste Lamarck (1744–1829). Lamarck believed in the evolution of species through the passing on of acquired characteristics. According to his theory, the fossils of extinct species represented not maladaptive species, but rather members of less adaptive versions of contemporary species (Hodge, 1990). The classic example of Lamarckian evolution is the giraffe, whose struggle to reach leaves on high branches resulted in an elongated neck, an acquired characteristic that was then passed on to its offspring.

Early in his career as a geologist and naturalist, Darwin was afforded an opportunity Lamarck and other scientists had not enjoyed: a trip on the HMS Beagle with Robert FitzRoy to observe nature on the coasts of South America (Meadows, 1987). It was during this trip that Darwin began to collect the observational data that served as evidence for the germination of his ideas about evolution as well as expertise in naturalist theory of his day.

While aboard the Beagle, Darwin read about and became sympathetic to the controversial views of the geologist, Charles Lyell (1797–1875). Lyell's *Principles of Geology* proposed an anti-Lamarckian notion of the nature of adaptation and extinction. Whereas Lamarck explained adaptation through the passing down of acquired characteristics and extinction as the result of poorly adapted characteristics, Lyell had a replacement theory of *adaptation* and extinction. Maladaptive species died out and were replaced by others that were better suited to the environment.

In contrast to these approaches to evolution, Darwin had a strong background in generational biology, which he had acquired under the tutelage of Robert G. Grant (1793–1874), from whom he learned to compare generations of species and to observe their commonalities and differences. This tendency to compare subsequent generations might lead a scientist toward a Lamarckian notion of a slow evolution of species; however, Lyell's notions about extinction were appealing to Darwin. Darwin was challenged to reconcile Lyell's notion that adaptation to the environment determines survival or extinction of an entire species with his Grantian knowledge of heredity as a result of sexual reproduction and his belief in the plausibility of transmutation, or modification, of species (Hodge, 1990).

In the years after digesting Lyell's book, Darwin began to integrate these distinct ideas into a new understanding of a genetically based notion of adaptation and extinction. Whereas Lyell claimed that maladaptive characteristics or change in environmental conditions caused a species to die out and be replaced by a superior one, Darwin proposed that species died out over time just as individuals do. Based on his observations of fossils, Darwin became convinced that differences in subsequent generations of species were not necessarily caused by differential adaptation, but could be due to genetic heritability, the transmutation of species over time (Hodge, 1990).

A few years later, Darwin happened upon a recent book by Thomas Malthus, his *Essay on the Principle of Population*. Malthus pointed out that extinction may be caused by competition for resources among individuals within a species. If it were not for competition, the demands of the large population would exceed the supply of natural resources. Whereas Lyell claimed competition between species, Malthus's discussion of populations gave Darwin an explanation for competition within species (Hodge, 1990). In addition, Darwin was reminded of selective breeding practiced by animal breeders. Those individuals with the most favorable characteristics could be selected and bred for specific traits. Realizing selection existed and that population grows so rapidly, Darwin suspected that sufficient variation could occur naturally, thus enabling natural selection to be an effective mechanism for evolution (Meadows, 1987).

Incorporating these new ideas into his theory, Darwin arrived at his theory of evolution through natural selection. Individuals within a species with the most adaptive characteristics are selected on the basis of competition in the population. The survival of these particular individuals ensures the propagation of successful genes in the next generation.

Darwin spent quite a bit of time formulating and perfecting his theories before they were eventually published in 1859 as his book *Origin of Species*. Previous to this publication, however, Alfred Russel Wallace (1823–1913) proposed a nearly identical concept of natural selection. The two thinkers presented their ideas together in 1858.

Darwin's theory was not a revolutionary concept that life has evolved from simple organisms and is continually being advanced through the mechanism of natural selection. Rather, Darwin's creative genius lay in his ability to selectively synthesize relevant aspects of various scientific perspectives into one concise theory. The revolutionary impact of Darwin's theory is most likely due to his "careful reasoning and mountain of observational evidence that the doctrine of the evolution of species by natural selection was a sound and plausible one" (Cohen, 1985, p. 291). Darwin did not propose a radically new idea, nor did he rehash previous proposals; rather, Darwin successfully stated a carefully synthesized theory whose implications led to a new era of scientific endeavor.

☐ Arts and Letters

Integration also applies in the arts and letters, as in literature. Ernest Becker's Pulitzer Prize–winning book *The Denial of Death* (1973) is an example of a text that integrates different fields (such as philosophy and psychology). Becker's book examined several different theorists, such as Sigmund Freud, Soren Kierkegaard, and Otto Rank, and interpreted them as actually centering on a fear of death. Becker analyzed Freud's theory, for example, and argued that Freud was actually writing about death, not sex. This analysis produced an acclaimed unified theory of human motivation, in which mankind constructs entire cultures as a mechanism of dealing with the fear of death (Becker, 1973).

Another example of an integration is *Fatherland*, Robert Harris's 1992 best-selling novel of historical speculation. The genre of historical speculation is one in which the author imagines a world different from the one we live in because of a fundamental change in history. One possibility is a world in which a famous event in the past did not occur (e.g., if John F. Kennedy had not been assassinated). Another possibility is a world in which an event that did not occur had, in fact, happened (e.g., if Adolf Hitler had been assassinated). In *Fatherland*, Harris conceptualizes a world in which Germany defeated the Allies in World War II. But rather than spending the majority of the book setting up the world and describing the "new" history, Harris plunges right in and begins a suspense thriller. Harris took the two genres—historical speculation and suspense thrillers—and fused them into a well-received novel.

Still another example of integration, this time in the domain of art, is in the innovative artwork of Rob Silvers. Silvers (1997) takes Georges Seurat's pointillist technique of using many small dots to form a larger work and combines it with the field of photography. Silvers uses thousands of tiny photographs and puts them together to form a larger image. His type of work, called photo mosaics, has become well known; Silvers designed the movie poster for *The Truman Show* and has created portraits of such disparate individuals as Princess Diana, Abraham Lincoln, and Darth Vader.

For another example of integration we can consider the classical music scene in the Jazz Age. At this time, many classical composers were sampling elements of the jazz idiom in their works, but the most successful integrator of jazz with the tradition of Western art music was a jazzman himself, George Gershwin. Gershwin's *Concerto in F* (1925), the follow-up to his increasingly popular *Rhapsody in Blue* of the previous year, successfully synthesized the world of popular jazz with the classical idiom. In this piece, Gershwin drew not only on syncopation and blues harmonies as he did in the *Rhapsody*, but also successfully synthesized these elements with classical concerto form. The first movement follows traditional sonata form in its statement and development of a few key themes.

Gershwin's contribution casts a new light on the field of music. Gershwin, a jazz pianist whose formal classical training began at age 14, succeeded in integrating into the tradition of art music the inclusion of popular elements (Schwartz, 1973). Until then, classical and popular idioms had been separated despite attempts of other composers to integrate the two. Schwartz (1980) has explained that "despite the many composers who have sought to emulate [Gershwin's] success by popularizing their operas and concert works, Gershwin has had little direct influence on other composers" (p. 303). This comment confirms that the *Concerto in F* was not an increment in art music—it was not a step leading down a long and prolific path in musical history. However, this piece was not a replication of any other jazz piece, or classical one, for that matter. The freshness of Gershwin's music caught the interest of many music lovers in the Jazz Age.

Robert Wright and George Forrest reached acclaim in musical theater for their synthesis of two different musical art forms. Wright and Forrest used a common technique in classical music, the variation, in which a composer takes another composer's music and writes his or her own variations on this theme. What Wright and Forrest did, however, was to transform the work of the composer Alexander Borodin not into a symphony or concerto but into a work of musical theater. Using Borodin's basic melodies, Wright and Forrest adapted a theatrical style and added lyrics, creating *Kismet*. This 1953 musical ran more than 500 performances and was a financial success, spawning the hit song "Stranger in Paradise." *Kismet* was merely the most well known example of Wright and Forrest's technique; their other "variation" musicals included *Song of Norway* (Grieg's music, 1944), *Gypsy Lady* (Herbert's music, 1946), *Magdalena* (Villa-Lobos's music, 1948), and *Anya* (Rachmaninoff's music, 1965) (Suskin, 1990, 1997).

☐ Popular Culture

Integrations are also found in the popular culture. Parody songs and records have always been popular—the music of "Weird Al" Yankovic is a well-known example of the genre, yet, quite naturally, it was assumed that the audience for parody songs would not overlap much with the sophisticated theatre crowd. While some parody songs may have used popular show tunes as their source, the idea of having a whole evening of theater parodies and spoofs could not have struck any potential producer as a profitable investment. And, indeed, when Gerard Alessandrini first mounted his show *Forbidden Broadway*, it was originally performed for a handful of people in a friend's living room. Yet soon after the show opened at a public place (Palsson's Upstairs Supper Club) in December 1981, the idea took off. The show became an off-Broadway smash. Indeed, Alessandrini kept periodically revising the show to keep up with the changing times (and briefly engineered another show in a similar vein, *Forbidden Hollywood*). The show has spawned six cast albums and is still running off-Broadway and touring across the United States. The various actors in the show have become more and more accomplished to the point where many of the Broadway shows that are spoofed today feature alumni of *Forbidden Broadway* in the cast. Broadway luminaries such as Ethel Merman (who saw the show shortly before she passed away) mostly enjoyed seeing themselves spoofed; when Carol Channing saw that she *was not* spoofed in the show, she called Alessandrini and asked to be spoofed, and she soon was (Barton, 2001).

Unlike most parody songs, the skits assume that the audience is intelligent and knowledgeable (references to an underbudgeted production of *Sweeney Todd* or a failed musicalization of *Anna Karenina* would not be understood by even many frequent theatergoers). And unlike many theater shows, *Forbidden Broadway* is not too highbrow to have jokes and songs that focus on people's embarrassing or nasty habits (such as Kevin Kline's accidental spitting while singing, Mandy Patinkin's occasionally over-the-top histrionics, or Elaine Stritch's tendencies to sing off-key and take her shoes off while on stage).

The show also often pokes fun at theater-attendance faux pas. One version of the show opened with a man and a woman apparently entering the theater late and loudly arguing over their seats. Just as enough members of the audience began staring at them (and, in some cases, saying "shhh"), they walk up on the stage and begin singing the show's theme song. Integrating the mass appeal of a great parody and the more refined pleasures of a show may not have been an obvious creative production, but it was certainly a successful one (Alessandrini, 1984).

Integration also applies in film. The concept of a musical about tough gangsters represents an integration of two fields in and of itself. The image of four Prohibition-era toughs stealing and harassing people does not usually result in those same four mobsters beginning to gleefully sing that they could have been anything they wanted to be, and yet they chose to "be bad." *Bugsy Malone* represents an integration of three different fields, because these four racketeers are played by children.

Alan Parker's *Bugsy Malone* is a gangster film, a musical, and a children's movie, all in one. Starring a young Jodie Foster and Scott Baio, *Bugsy Malone* tells a traditional gangland story of two rival mobs, one led by "Dandy Dan" and the other led by "Fat Sam," and their competition over a new type of weapon. Woven into the story is the title character, who is a charming loner; an aspiring singer named Blousey; and Talullah, a seductive chanteuse. Having this story told as a movie musical represents an integration, but one that has its origins on stage. (*Guys and Dolls* and *Happy End*, while not traditional gangster tales, nonetheless used similar ideas.) But the truly original propulsion occurred when Parker took a type of children's movie, exemplified by the *Our Gang* and *Little Rascals* series with children as the main characters, and integrated this genre with his gangster musical. The weapon that the two rival gangs were fighting over, for example? It is a large gun that shoots out cream pies.

Two of the most popular science fiction creations represent similar integrations of different fields. Gene Roddenberry's *Star Trek* and George Lucas's *Star Wars* both were able to integrate the fields of science fiction and westerns. *Star Trek* was a television show that was based on a concept similar to the western show *Wagon Train*—sturdy and resilient men and women prevailed over an assortment of people. In *Star Trek*, humans and Vulcans triumphed over a variety of alien species (Panati, 1991). In a similar vein, George Lucas used a famous western plot in a science fiction setting. The basic story of *Star Wars* closely mirrors the plot of the John Wayne classic *The Searchers*; again, however, the setting of the Old West is replaced by outer space. *Star Wars* also integrates the field of Japanese Samurai movies; the plot of *Star Wars: A New Hope* is reminiscent of *Kakushi Toride no San Akunin* (1958). The character of Obi-Wan Kenobi can be seen to represent a Samurai warrior, while the two robots R2-D2 and C-3PO resemble two crooks who were hired to help rescue a princess in the original Japanese movie.

Consider integration as it applies in politics. Barry Goldwater integrated two very different facets of conservatism in his groundbreaking political tract *The Conscience of a Conservative* (1960). Goldwater (who was greatly helped with the book by Brent Bozell) bridged the gap between traditional conservatives and libertarian conservatives by appealing to aspects of both philosophies. He argued, for example, that the New Deal was a move toward totalitarianism, and that the government should not be active in most aspects of life—yet he also argued in favor of the government's need to sustain order and reinforce morality. He brought together the two different conservative factions by uniting them on the goal of fighting communism. Goldwater's ability to bring two very different types of conservative ideologies together helped establish conservatism as a strong force from the 1960s to the present day (Dalek, 1995).

Integration applies also to social movements. When Maggie Kuhn was forced to retire from her position with the Presbyterian Church when she reached the mandatory retirement age of 65 in 1971, she decided to fight back against the system that was making her leave her job. While there were already some groups that existed to defend the rights of elderly people, none of them had a great deal of impact on policy making. Kuhn integrated the techniques of forceful civil rights groups such as the Black Panthers with the goals of these early ageism-fighting groups. In honor of the Black Panthers, Kuhn and the early leaders dubbed their group the Gray Panthers.

The Gray Panthers began to spread the idea that the elderly had to become actively involved in their own lives. If older people did not want to be condescended or disregarded, they had to work for more respect and rights, just as the Black Panthers and other 1960s civil rights groups did. Because of the efforts of the Gray Panthers, mandatory retirement laws were mostly ended, nursing homes were reformed on a national level, and widespread fraud and scams aimed at the elderly were fought. Kuhn herself stayed active with the group until her death at 89; the Gray Panthers' ranks have swelled to as many as 60,000, and their impact is strongly felt today (Kuhn, Long, & Quinn, 1991).

An example of a historical integration is the complex evolution of the Japanese written language. Originally, Japanese was strictly a spoken language, but around 500 A.D., Japanese speakers began to use Chinese *kanji* (pictographs) to represent Japanese words. While written Japanese looked identical to the Chinese, any one character was pronounced in two different ways, one of which approximated the Chinese pronunciation, and the other of which corresponded to the Japanese word bearing the same meaning. Since 1945, close to 2,000 kanji have been designated as Kanji for Daily Use in the Japanese language. These are the kanji that children learn in school today (Miyagawa, 2000).

By 1000 A.D., however, the Japanese needed a supplemental system to represent Japanese words that had no Chinese counterpart. To meet this purpose, syllabaries called *kana* were derived from Chinese characters. Rather than representing the meaning of a whole word, a kana represents a syllable or sound. There are two systems of kana in modern Japanese. The first, called *hiragana*, originated with Buddhist priests, who while translating Chinese works into Japanese began inserting syllables next to characters to designate a particular Japanese inflection or alternate meaning from the Chinese (Vogler, 1998). The second system of kana, *katakana*, is primarily used to represent foreign words.

The original use of Chinese characters to represent Japanese words may be viewed as a redefinition of sorts. That is, the meaning remained the same while the label, or way of reaching that meaning, changed. However, the entire Japanese language is best seen as an integration (and subsequent forward incrementation) of symbol systems. Specifically, the introduction of kana to modify kanji is a particularly good example of melding two representational systems into one entirely new system. The meanings of words with kanji and kana are not fully decipherable based solely on the kanji, evidence that a true integration has taken place.

In sum, integration occurs when creators synthesize two or more paradigms, whether two old ones, an old one and a new one, or, rarely, two new ones. Of course, we are not the first to speak of such syntheses. It thus is an appropriate time to discuss how our model relates to theories of the past, which have contained related ideas.

10
CHAPTER

The Relation of the Propulsion
Model to Theories of Creativity

How does the propulsion model relate to other views on creativity? In this chapter, we review briefly some of the history of the study of creativity (see Albert & Runco, 1999, for more details). In our analysis (based in large part on Sternberg & Lubart, 1996, 1999), we consider some of the main approaches to studying creativity, including mystical, pragmatic, psychoanalytic, psychometric, cognitive, and social-personality approaches. We then consider what we believe to be the most promising approach for future work on creativity, the confluence approach. In discussing each approach, we attempt to discuss its relation to our proposed propulsion model.

☐ Mystical Approaches

The study of creativity has always been tinged—some might say tainted—with associations with mystical beliefs. Perhaps the earliest accounts of creativity were based on divine intervention. The creative person was seen as an empty vessel that a divine being would fill with inspiration. The individual would then pour out the inspired ideas, forming an otherworldly product.

In this vein, Plato argued that a poet is able to create only that which the Muse dictates, and even today people sometimes refer to their own Muse as a source of inspiration. In Plato's view, one person might be inspired to create choral songs, another, epic poems (Rothenberg & Hausman, 1976). Often, mystical sources have been suggested in creators' introspective reports (Ghiselin, 1985). For example, Rudyard Kipling referred to the "Daemon" that lives in the writer's pen: "My Daemon was with me in the Jungle Books, Kim, and both Puck books, and good care I took to walk delicately, lest he should withdraw. . . . When your Daemon is in charge, do not think consciously. Drift, wait, and obey" (Kipling, 1937/1985, p. 162).

The mystical approach can probably apply to any of the different kinds of creativity, and so it is necessary to analyze particular "mystical events" rather than all possible mystical events that might occur. The approach takes a slightly more grounded form when it is linked, for example, to dreams. A well-known example of such a dream is one described by the scientist Poincaré, who described himself as having discovered the ring-like chemical structure of benzene in a dream when he envisioned a snake dancing around and biting its tail. This discovery was a forward incrementation, a vital next step that eluded the scientist until the night of his dream. The poem *Kubla Khan* was also supposed to have been written in a trancelike state (or so Coleridge said), and it, too, represented a forward incrementation on existing forms of poetry (even if the alleged experience of creating it did not!).

The mystical approaches to the study of creativity have probably made it harder for scientists to be heard. Many people seem to believe, as they believe for love (see Sternberg, 1988a, 1988b), that creativity is something that just does not lend itself to scientific study, because it is a more spiritual process. We believe that it has been difficult for scientific work to shake the deep-seated view of some that, somehow, scientists are treading where they should not.

☐ Pragmatic Approaches

Pragmatic approaches have been concerned primarily with developing creativity, secondarily with understanding it, but almost not at all with testing the validity of ideas about the nature of creativity (see Sternberg & Lubart, 1996).

Perhaps the foremost proponent of this approach is Edward De Bono, whose work on *lateral thinking*—seeing things broadly and from varied viewpoints—as well as other aspects of creativity has had what appears to be considerable commercial success (e.g., DeBono, 1971, 1985, 1992). Lateral thinking should, in theory, yield redirections, as the idea is to veer 90 degrees off one's current direction in order to generate creative ideas.

In all likelihood, however, few of the ideas it yields truly are redirections, although we cannot be certain.

DeBono's concern is not with theory, but with practice. Thus, for example, he suggests using a tool such as PMI to focus on the aspects of an idea that are pluses, minuses, and interesting. Or he suggests using the word "po," derived from *hypothesis, suppose, possible,* and *poetry,* to provoke rather than judge ideas. Another tool, that of "thinking hats," has individuals metaphorically wear different hats, such as a white hat for data-based thinking, a red hat for intuitive thinking, a black hat for critical thinking, and a green hat for generative thinking, in order to stimulate seeing things from different points of view. The use of thinking hats seems most likely to generate integrative ideas, that is, ideas that integrate the variety of different viewpoints represented by the hats of the different colors.

DeBono is not alone in this enterprise. Osborn (1953), based on his experiences in advertising agencies, developed the technique of brainstorming to encourage people to solve problems creatively by seeking many possible solutions in an atmosphere that is constructive rather than critical and inhibitory. Gordon (1961) developed synectics, which involves primarily seeing analogies, also for stimulating creative thinking. Analogies are often integrative in nature, because they relate the new domain in which one is working to some old domain one previously has studied.

More recently, authors such as Adams (1974, 1986) and von Oech (1983) have suggested that people often construct a series of false beliefs that interfere with creative functioning. For example, some people believe that there is only one *right* answer and that ambiguity must be avoided whenever possible. People can become creative by identifying and removing these mental blocks. von Oech (1986) has also suggested that to be creative we need to adopt the roles of explorer, artist, judge, and warrior to foster our creative productivity. The different roles may yield different kinds of creativity. For example, the warrior fights against existing ideas and, if successful, breaks existing paradigms to generate redirective and reinitiative ideas.

These approaches have had considerable public visibility, in much the same way that Leo Buscaglia gave visibility to the study of love. And they may well be useful. From our point of view as psychologists, however, the approaches lack any basis in serious psychological theory as well as serious empirical attempts to validate them. Of course, techniques can work in the absence of psychological theory or validation. It is therefore important not to reject the ideas because they have not been proposed or fully studied in a scientific context.

☐ The Psychodynamic Approach

The psychodynamic approach can be considered the first of the major twentieth-century theoretical approaches to the study of creativity. Based on the idea that creativity arises from the tension between conscious reality and unconscious drives, Freud (1908/1959) proposed that writers and artists produce creative work as a way to express their unconscious wishes in a publicly acceptable fashion. These unconscious wishes may concern power, riches, fame, honor, or love (Vernon, 1970). Case studies of eminent creators, such as Leonardo da Vinci (Freud, 1910/1964), were used to support these ideas. Indeed, Freud said that "We laymen have always been curious to know . . . from what source that strange being, the creative writer, draws his material, and how he manages to make such an impression on us with it" (p. 143).

Later, the psychoanalytic approach introduced the concepts of adaptive regression and elaboration for creativity (Kris, 1952). *Adaptive regression*, the primary process, refers to the intrusion of unmodulated thoughts in consciousness. Unmodulated thoughts can occur during active problem solving, but often occur during sleep, intoxication from drugs, fantasies or daydreams, or psychoses. *Elaboration*, the secondary process, refers to the reworking and transformation of primary-process material through reality-oriented, ego-controlled thinking. Other theorists (e.g., Kubie, 1958) emphasized that the preconscious, which falls between conscious reality and the encrypted unconscious, is the true source of creativity because thoughts are loose and vague but interpretable. In contrast to Freud, Kubie claimed that unconscious conflicts actually have a negative effect on creativity because they lead to fixated, repetitive thoughts. Recent work has recognized the importance of both primary and secondary process (Noy, 1969; Rothenberg, 1979; Suler, 1980; Werner & Kaplan, 1963).

Adaptive regression and related concepts may yield various kinds of creativity, but they seem oriented at relieving one of the constraints that conscious, secondary-process thought places on one's thinking, and hence they seem most oriented toward thinking that breaks out of existing molds, at least with respect to oneself. So the resulting creativity may be paradigm breaking, not necessarily with respect to one's field, but with respect to oneself.

Although the psychodynamic approach may have offered some insights into creativity, psychodynamic theory was not at the center of the emerging scientific psychology. The early twentieth century schools of psychology, such as structuralism, functionalism, and behaviorism, were devoting practically no resources at all to the study of creativity. The Gestaltists studied a portion of creativity—insight—but their study never went much beyond labeling, as opposed to characterizing the nature of insight.

Further isolating creativity research, the psychodynamic approach and other early work on creativity relied on case studies of eminent creators. This methodology has been criticized historically because of the difficulty of measuring proposed theoretical constructs (such as primary process thought), and the amount of selection and interpretation that can occur in a case study (Weisberg, 1993). Although there is nothing a priori wrong with case study methods, the emerging scientific psychology valued controlled experimental methods. Thus both theoretical and methodological issues served to isolate the study of creativity from mainstream psychology.

☐ Psychometric Approaches

When we think of creativity, eminent artists or scientists such as Michelangelo or Einstein immediately come to mind. However, these highly creative people are quite rare and difficult to study in the psychological laboratory. In his APA address, Guilford (1950) noted that these problems had limited research on creativity. He proposed that creativity could be studied in everyday subjects using paper-and-pencil tasks. One of these was the Unusual Uses Test (also called the Alternative Uses Test), in which an examinee thinks of as many uses for a common object (such as a brick) as possible. Many researchers adopted Guilford's suggestion and "divergent thinking" tasks quickly became the main instruments for measuring creative thinking. The tests were a convenient way of comparing people on a standard "creativity" scale. They were, however, rather close in nature to some intelligence tests.

Building on Guilford's work, Torrance (1974) developed the *Torrance Tests of Creative Thinking*. These tests consist of several relatively simple verbal and figural tasks that involve divergent thinking plus other problem-solving skills. The tests can be scored for fluency (total number of relevant responses), flexibility (number of different categories of relevant responses), originality (the statistical rarity of the responses), and elaboration (amount of detail in the responses). Some subtests from the Torrance battery include:

1. Asking questions: The examinee writes out all the questions he or she can think of, based on a drawing of a scene.
2. Product improvement: The examinee lists ways to change a toy monkey so that children will have more fun playing with it.
3. Unusual uses: The examinee lists interesting and unusual uses of a cardboard box.

4. Circles: The examinee expands empty circles into different drawings and titles them.

Catherine Cox (1926), working with Lewis Terman, believed that exceptionally creative people are also exceptionally intelligent. She published IQ estimates for 301 of the most eminent persons who lived between 1450 and 1850. They selected their group from a list of 1,000 prepared by James McKeen Cattell, who determined eminence by the amount of space allotted in biographical dictionaries. From Cattell's list, they deleted hereditary aristocracy and nobility unless those individuals distinguished themselves beyond status due to their birth, those born before 1450, those with a rank over 510 on the original list, and 11 names for whom no records were available. These deletions left 282 persons whose IQs were summarized as Group A. In addition, they discussed a Group B, which consisted of 19 miscellaneous cases from those over 510 on the original list, bringing the grand total to 301.

To estimate IQ, Cox, Terman, and Maud Merrill (Cox, 1926) examined biographies, letters, and other writings and records for evidence of the earliest period of instruction; the nature of the earliest learning; the earliest productions; age of first reading and of first mathematical performance; typical precocious activities; unusually intelligent applications of knowledge; the recognition of similarities or differences; the amount and character of the reading; the range of interests; school standing and progress; early maturity of attitude or judgment; the tendency to discriminate, to generalize, or to theorize; and family standing. Their IQ estimates are, of course, necessarily subjective. In a sense, though, the estimates have an ecological validity with regard to real-life intelligence that is not seen in standard IQ tests. The reported IQs were the average of the three expert raters mentioned above, namely, Cox, Terman, and Merrill. Interrater reliability was .90 for the childhood estimate and .89 for the young adulthood estimate (calculated from intercorrelations in Cox, 1926, pp. 67–68).

An example of some of the factors that contributed to their estimates can be seen in a description of Francis Galton (not on the list; he was born in 1822 and published *Hereditary Genius* in 1869), whose IQ Terman estimated to be 200. "Francis knew his capital letters by twelve months and both his alphabets by eighteen months; . . . he could read a little book, *Cobwebs to Catch Flies*, when 2½ years old, and could sign his name before 3 years" (Cox, 1926, pp. 41–42). By 4 years of age, he could say all the Latin substantives and adjectives and active verbs, could add and multiply, read a little French, and knew the clock. At 5, he was quoting from Walter Scott. By 6, he was familiar with the *Iliad* and the *Odyssey*. At 7, he was reading Shakespeare for fun and could memorize a page by reading it twice. Clearly, Galton's record is one of an exceptional child.

Cox concluded that the average IQs of the group, 135 for childhood and 145 for young adulthood, were probably too low because of instructions to regress toward the mean of 100 for unselected populations (whereas this group's means were 135 and 145) whenever data were unavailable. Also, unreliability of the data may have caused regression to the mean. One of the problems Cox noted in the data was a strong correlation, .77, between IQ and the reliability of the available data: The more reliable the data, the higher the IQ, and the higher the IQ, the more reliable the data upon which it was based. She concluded that if more reliable data had been available, all of the IQs would have been estimated to be higher. She therefore corrected the original estimates, bringing the group average up to 155 for childhood and 165 for young adulthood.

As Cox was careful to point out, the IQs are not estimates of the actual person's IQ, but, rather, are estimates of the record of that person: "The IQ of Newton or of Lincoln recorded in these pages is the IQ of the Newton or of the Lincoln of whom we have record. But the records are admittedly incomplete" (Cox, 1926, p. 8). Moreover, the estimates of IQ are largely verbal, as they are based on Binet and Simon's (1916) conception of intelligence, prior to the introduction of the more balanced conception of Wechsler (1939), which recognized nonverbal skills more.

Cox found the correlation between IQ and rank order of eminence to be .16, plus or minus .039 (Cox, 1926, p. 55), after correcting for unreliability of the data. Dean Simonton (1976) reexamined the Cox data using multiple regression techniques. He showed that the correlation between intelligence and ranked eminence that Cox found was an artifact of unreliability of data and, especially, of a timewise sampling bias—those more recently born had both lower estimated IQs and lower ranks of estimated eminence. In Simonton's analysis, the relationship between intelligence and ranked eminence was zero if birth year was controlled for (Simonton, 1976, pp. 223–224). In any case, Cox recognized the role of factors other than IQ in eminence and concluded that "high but not the highest intelligence, combined with the greatest degree of persistence, will achieve greater eminence than the highest degree of intelligence with somewhat less persistence" (Cox, 1926, p. 187).

Three basic findings concerning conventional conceptions of intelligence as measured by IQ and creativity are generally agreed upon (see, e.g., Barron & Harrington, 1981; Lubart, 1994; Sternberg & O'Hara, 1999). First, creative people tend to show above-average IQs, often above 120 (see Renzulli, 1986). This figure is not a cutoff, but rather an expression of the fact that people with low or even average IQs do not seem to be well represented among the ranks of highly creative individuals. Simonton (1999) has suggested that lower IQ thus may set a limit on how creative one can be. Cox's (1926) geniuses had an estimated average IQ of 165.

Barron estimated the mean IQ of his creative writers to be 140 or higher, based on their scores on the Terman Concept Mastery Test (Barron, 1963, p. 242). It should be noted that the Concept Mastery Test is exclusively verbal, and thus provides a somewhat skewed estimate of IQ. The other groups in the University of California Berkeley Institute for Personality Assessment Research (IPAR) studies, that is, mathematicians and research scientists, were also above average in intelligence. Anne Roe (1952, 1972), who performed similarly thorough assessments of eminent scientists before the IPAR group was formed, estimated IQs for her participants that ranged between 121 and 194, with medians between 137 and 166, depending on whether the IQ test was verbal, spatial, or mathematical.

Second, above an IQ of 120, IQ does not seem to matter as much to creativity as it does below 120. In other words, creativity may be more highly correlated with IQ below a level of 120, but only weakly or not at all correlated with it above an IQ of 120. (This relationship is often called the threshold theory. See the contrast with Hayes's [1989] certification theory discussed below.) In the architects' study, in which the average IQ was 130 (significantly above average), the correlation between intelligence and creativity was −.08, not significantly different from zero (Barron, 1969, p. 42). But in the military officer study, in which participants were of average intelligence, the correlation was .33 (Barron, 1963, p. 219). These results suggest that extremely highly creative people often have high IQs, but not necessarily that people with high IQs tend to be extremely creative (see also Getzels & Jackson, 1962).

Some investigators (e.g., Simonton, 1994; Sternberg, 1996) have suggested that very high IQ may actually interfere with creativity. Those who have very high IQs may be so highly rewarded for their IQ-like (analytical) skills that they fail to develop the creative potential within them, which may then remain latent. In a reexamination of the Cox (1926) data, Simonton (1976) found that the eminent leaders showed a significant negative correlation, −.29, between their IQs and eminence. Simonton (1976) explained,

> Leaders must be understood by a large mass of people before they can achieve eminence, unlike the creators, who need only appeal to an intellectual elite. . . . Scientific, philosophical, literary, artistic, and musical creators do not have to achieve eminence in their own lifetime to earn posterity's recognition, whereas military, political, or religious leaders must have contemporary followers to attain eminence. (pp. 220, 222)

Third, the correlation between IQ and creativity is variable, usually ranging from weak to moderate (Flescher, 1963; Getzels & Jackson, 1962; Guilford, 1967; Herr, Moore, & Hasen, 1965; Torrance, 1962; Wallach & Kogan, 1965; Yamamoto, 1964). The correlation depends in part upon what aspects of creativity and intelligence are being measured and how they are being measured as well as in what field the creativity is manifested. The role of intelligence is different in art and music, for instance, than it is in mathematics and science (McNemar, 1964).

An obvious drawback to the tests used and assessments done by Roe and Guilford is the time and expense involved in administering them as well as the subjective scoring of them. In contrast, Mednick (1962) produced a 30-item, objectively scored, 40-minute test of creative ability called the Remote Associates Test (RAT). The test is based on his theory that the creative thinking process is the forming of associative elements into new combinations that either meet specified requirements or are in some way useful. The more mutually remote the elements of the new combination, according to Mednick, the more creative the process or solution. Because the ability to make these combinations and arrive at a creative solution necessarily depends on the existence of the stuff of the combinations, that is, the associative elements, in a person's knowledge base and because the probability and speed of attainment of a creative solution are influenced by the organization of the person's associations, Mednick's theory suggests that creativity and intelligence are very related; they are overlapping sets.

The RAT requires that the test-taker supply a fourth word that is remotely associated with three given words. Samples (not actual test items) of given words follow:

1. rat   blue   cottage
2. surprise   line   birthday
3. out   dog   cat

(Answers are *1. cheese, 2. party, 3. house.*)

Moderate correlations of .55, .43, and .41 have been shown between the RAT and the Wechsler Intelligence Scale for Children (WISC), the SAT verbal, and the Lorge-Thorndike Verbal Intelligence measures, respectively (Mednick & Andrews, 1967). Correlations with quantitative intelligence measures were lower (r = .20–.34). Correlations with other measures of creative performance have been more variable (Andrews, 1975).

In our view, psychometric approaches stressing divergent thinking measure the potential to diverge (redirect or reinitiate), but at such microlevels of creative thought that it is not clear that there will be much transfer to serious work in a professional field of endeavor. Thinking of unusual uses of a paperclip, for example, does not seem particularly close to thinking of unusual ways of studying quantum-physical phenomena, human creativity, or other serious disciplinary problems.

This argument suggests that in addition to kind of creativity and quality of creative ideas, we need to think in terms of scope of creative ideas. People who are seriously creative in their work are those who are more likely to deal with problems of larger rather than smaller scope. The ideas that are sufficiently remembered to become a part of human cultural history are remembered in part because they deal with problems that people care about. It may be for this reason that creativity tests, and even intelligence tests, do not provide more than modest prediction of major intellectual or creative endeavors. The scope of the problems in these tests is just too small. This analysis does not imply that such tests are useless, but, rather, only that they may be useful in predicting creativity locally rather than globally.

The psychometric revolution for measuring creativity had both positive and negative effects on the field. On the positive side, the tests facilitated research by providing a brief, easy-to-administer assessment device that can be objectively scored. Furthermore, research was now possible with "everyday" people (i.e., noneminent samples). However, there were some negative effects as well. First, some researchers criticized brief paper-and-pencil tests as trivial, inadequate measures of creativity; larger productions such as actual drawings or writing samples should be used instead. Second, other critics suggested that none of the fluency, flexibility, originality, and elaboration scores captured the concept of creativity. In fact, the definition and criteria for creativity are a matter of ongoing debate and relying on the objectively defined statistical rarity of a response with regard to all the responses of a subject population is only one of many options. Other possibilities include using the social consensus of judges. Third, some researchers rejected the assumption that noneminent samples could shed light on eminent levels of creativity, which was the ultimate goal of many studies of creativity. Thus a certain malaise developed and continues to accompany the paper-and-pencil assessment of creativity. Some psychologists, at least, avoided this measurement quagmire in favor of less problematic research topics.

☐ Cognitive Approaches

The cognitive approach to creativity seeks understanding of the mental representations and processes underlying creative thought. By studying, say, perception, or memory, one would already be studying the bases of creativity; thus, the study of creativity would merely represent an extension, and perhaps not a very large one, of work that is already being done under another guise. For example, in the cognitive area, creativity was often subsumed under the study of intelligence. We do not argue with the idea that creativity and intelligence are related to each other. However, the subsumption has often been so powerful that researchers such as Wallach and Kogan (1965), among others, had to write at length on why creativity and intelligence should be viewed as distinct entities. In more recent cognitive work, Weisberg (1986, 1988, 1993, 1999) has proposed that creativity involves essentially ordinary cognitive processes yielding extraordinary products. Weisberg attempted to show that the insights depend on subjects using conventional cognitive processes (such as analogical transfer) applied to knowledge already stored in memory. He did so through the use of case studies of eminent creators and laboratory research, such as studies with Duncker's (1945) candle problem. This problem requires participants to attach a candle to a wall using only objects available in a picture (candle, box of tacks, and book of matches). Langley and colleagues (1987) made a similar claim about the ordinary nature of creative thinking.

As a concrete example of this approach, Weisberg and Alba (1981) had people solve the notorious nine-dot problem. In this problem, people are asked to connect all of the dots, which are arranged in the shape of a square with three rows of three dots each, using no more than four straight lines, never arriving at a given dot twice, and never lifting their pencil from the page. The problem can be solved only if people allow their line segments to go outside the periphery of the dots. Typically, solution of this task had been viewed as hinging upon the insight that one had to go "outside the box." Weisberg and Alba showed that even when people were given the insight, they still had difficulty in solving the problem. In other words, whatever is required to solve the nine-dot problem, it is not just some kind of extraordinary insight.

This view implies that, whatever the kind of creativity one shows, it is more a function of knowledge than of any special kind of information processing. We are skeptical of this view. We believe that Weisberg may be correct, in large part, with regard to replicatory and forward-incremental contributions. These contributions make heavy use of past work, and the better one knows and understands the past work, the better the position one is in to advance beyond this work in the direction the work is already leading. But even though knowledge may be necessary for creativity, it is not sufficient, and it may be as likely to interfere with paradigm-breaking ideas as to facilitate them (Sternberg & Lubart, 1995).

There have been studies with both human subjects and computer simulations of creative thought. Approaches based on the study of human subjects are perhaps prototypically exemplified by the work of Finke, Ward, and Smith (1992; see also contributions to Smith, Ward, & Finke, 1995; Sternberg & Davidson, 1994; Ward, Smith, & Finke, 1999). Finke and his colleagues have proposed what they call the *Geneplore model*, according to which there are two main processing phases in creative thought: a generative phase and an exploratory phase. In the generative phase, an individual constructs mental representations referred to as preinventive structures, which have properties promoting creative discoveries. In the exploratory phase, these properties are used to come up with creative ideas. A number of mental processes may enter into these phases of creative invention, such as retrieval, association, synthesis, transformation, analogical transfer, and categorical reduction (i.e., mentally reducing objects or elements to more primitive categorical descriptions). In a typical experimental test based on the model (see, e.g., Finke, 1990), participants will be shown parts of objects, such as a circle, a cube, a parallelogram, and a cylinder. On a given trial, three parts will be named, and participants will be asked to imagine combining the parts to produce a practical object or device. In terms of the propulsion model, this kind of creativity is integrative in character. For example, participants might imagine a tool, a weapon, or a piece of furniture. The objects thus produced are then rated by judges for their practicality and originality.

The goal of computer-simulation approaches, reviewed by Boden (1992, 1999), is to produce creative thought in a manner that simulates how people think. Langley, Simon, Bradshaw, and Zytkow (1987), for example, developed a set of programs that rediscover basic scientific laws. These computational models rely on heuristics—problem-solving guidelines—for searching a data set or conceptual space and finding hidden relationships between input variables. The initial program, called BACON, uses heuristics such as "if the value of two numerical terms increase together, consider their ratio" to search data for patterns. One of BACON's accomplishments has been to examine observational data on the orbits of planets available to Kepler and to rediscover Kepler's third law of planetary motion. This program is unlike creative functioning, however, in that the problems are given to it in structured form, whereas creative functioning is largely about figuring out what the problems are.

There are also models concerning an artistic domain. For example, Johnson-Laird (1988) developed a jazz improvisation program in which novel deviations from the basic jazz chord sequences are guided by harmonic constraints (or tacit principles of jazz) and random choice when several allowable directions for the improvisation exist.

☐ Social-Personality Approaches

Developing in parallel with the cognitive approach, work in the social-personality approach has focused on personality variables, motivational variables, and the sociocultural environment as sources of creativity. Researchers such as Amabile (1983), Barron (1968, 1969), Eysenck (1993),

Gough (1979), MacKinnon (1965), and others have noted that certain personality traits often characterize creative people. Through correlational studies and research contrasting high- and low-creative samples (at both eminent and everyday levels), a large set of potentially relevant traits has been identified (Barron & Harrington, 1981). These traits include independence of judgment, self-confidence, attraction to complexity, aesthetic orientation, openness to experience, psychoticism, and risk taking.

The particular constellation of personality traits one shows may determine the kind of creativity one is most likely to show. For example, someone who shows many of the creative personality traits but is not a risk taker is much more likely to show paradigm-accepting rather than paradigm-breaking forms of creativity. People who are highly agreeable or less independent also may be likely to prefer paradigm-accepting work. Higher degrees of psychoticism may increase individuals' social isolation and isolation from trends followed by colleagues, and increase the chances of paradigm-breaking work. Similarly, the oppositional nature found in some creative people may also increase the chances that these people will do paradigm-breaking work. In no case are personality traits likely to be *sufficient* for certain kinds of creative contributions. But they may be associated with such contributions or even, in some cases, necessary for them.

Proposals regarding self-actualization and creativity also can be considered within the personality tradition. According to Maslow (1968), boldness, courage, freedom, spontaneity, self-acceptance, and other traits lead a person to realize his or her full potential. Rogers (1954) described the tendency toward self-actualization as having motivational force and being promoted by a supportive, evaluation-free environment. Maslow and Rogers portrayed self-actualizing people as freeing themselves from the need to conform—to attain self-acceptance by achieving acceptance by others. People who self-actualize, therefore, may be in a better position to break out of existing paradigms than people who do not, and who need others' approval in order to approve of themselves.

Focusing on motivation for creativity, a number of theorists have hypothesized the relevance of intrinsic motivation (Amabile, 1983, 1996; Crutchfield, 1962; Golann, 1962), need for order (Barron, 1963), need for achievement (McClelland, Atkinson, Clark, & Lowell, 1953), and other motives. Amabile (1983; Hennessey & Amabile, 1988) and her colleagues have conducted seminal research on intrinsic and extrinsic motivation. Studies using motivational training and other techniques have manipulated these motivations and observed effects on creative performance tasks, such as writing poems and making collages.

People who are extrinsically motivated seem less likely to make paradigm-breaking contributions than people who are intrinsically motivated. The reason is that paradigm-breaking contributions, because they defy the crowd, often result not in extrinsic rewards but, rather, in extrinsic punishments. Intrinsically motivated people do what they do for the sake of their love of what they are doing. In their relative immunity to extrinsic considerations, they may be more likely to break out of existing paradigms and be more likely to accept the sometimes adverse consequences if they do.

Finally, the relevance of the social environment to creativity has also been an active area of research. At the societal level, Simonton (1984, 1988, 1994, 1999) has conducted numerous studies in which eminent levels of creativity over large spans of time in diverse cultures have been statistically linked to environmental variables. These variables include, among others, cultural diversity, war, availability of role models, availability of resources (such as financial support), and number of competitors in a domain. Cross-cultural comparisons (e.g., Lubart, 1990) and anthropological case studies (e.g., Maduro, 1976; Silver, 1981) have demonstrated cultural variability in the expression of creativity. Moreover, they have shown that cultures differ simply in the amount that they value the creative enterprise.

We believe that social-cultural variables may be strongly linked to kinds of creative contributions. A society that highly stresses conformity and acceptance of group norms is not likely to produce paradigm-breaking work. One of us has visited such a society, Singapore, on two occasions. In Singapore, the desire to be part of the common culture is strong, and this desire has, in many ways, worked to Singapore's advantage. The society has transformed itself from a minor part of Malaysia to a major world-class economic power in a matter of a few decades. But there also have been costs, namely, fear of creativity. Some of these costs are quite real, because there are penalties in Singapore for nonconforming behavior (such as a multitude of fines and the very real threat of lawsuits) that might not be found in many other places. The lesson to be learned, perhaps, is that the norms that lead to certain advantages may lead to other disadvantages, particularly with regard to creativity. If people are afraid of the consequences of creativity, and with just cause, they are simply less likely to be creative.

The cognitive and social-personality approaches each have provided valuable insights into creativity. However, if you look for research that investigates both cognitive and social-personality variables at the same time, you would find only a handful of studies. The cognitive work on creativity has tended to ignore the personality and social system, and the social-personality approaches tended to have little or nothing to say about the mental representations and processes underlying creativity.

Looking beyond the field of psychology, Wehner, Csikszentmihalyi, and Magyari-Beck (1991) examined 100 recent doctoral dissertations on creativity. They found a "parochial isolation" of the various studies concerning creativity. There were relevant dissertations from psychology, education, business, history, history of science, and other fields, such as sociology and political science. However, the different fields tended to use different terms and focus on different aspects of what seemed to be the same basic phenomenon. For example, business dissertations used the term "innovation" and tended to look at the organizational level, whereas psychology dissertations used "creativity" and looked at the level of the individual. Wehner, Csikszentmihalyi, and Magyari-Beck (1991) describe the situation with creativity research in terms of the fable of the blind men and the elephant: "We touch different parts of the same beast and derive distorted pictures of the whole from what we know: 'The elephant is like a snake,' says the one who only holds its tail; 'The elephant is like a wall,' says the one who touches its flanks" (p. 270).

☐ Evolutionary Approaches

The evolutionary approach to creativity was instigated by Donald Campbell (1960), who suggested that the same kinds of mechanisms that have been applied to the study of the evolution of organisms could be applied to the evolution of ideas. This idea has been enthusiastically adopted by a number of investigators (Perkins, 1995; Simonton, 1995, 1998, 1999).

The fundamental idea underlying this approach is that there are two basic steps in the generation and propagation of creative ideas. The first is *blind* variation, by which the creator generates an idea without any real idea of whether the idea will be successful (selected for) in the world of ideas. Indeed, Dean K. Simonton (1996) has argued that creators do not have the slightest idea of which of their ideas will succeed. As a result, their best bet for producing lasting ideas is to go for a large quantity of ideas. The reason is that their hit rate remains relatively constant through their professional life span. In other words, they have a fixed proportion of ideas that will succeed. The more ideas they have, the more ideas they have that will achieve success.

The second step is *selective retention*. In this step, the field in which the creator works either retains the idea for the future or lets it die out. Those ideas that are selectively retained are the ones that are judged to be novel and of value, that is, creative. This process as well as the process of blind generation are described further by Cziko (1998).

An evolutionary process of creativity does not imply any particular kind of creativity. Presumably, some evolutionary variations are small and incremental, whereas others are radical and qualitatively distinct from what has come before. Whether they succeed will depend upon their compatibility with the context in which they occur. In the case of the evolution of ideas, this context will be cultural. The audience constituting a cultural context may or may not be ready for a given innovation.

Does an evolutionary model really adequately describe creativity? Robert Sternberg (1997) has argued that it does not, and David Perkins (1998) also has expressed doubts. Sternberg argues that it seems utterly implausible that great creators such as Mozart, Einstein, or Picasso were using nothing more than blind variation to come up with their ideas. And the potential search space is so large that it is unclear how one could ever get to the point of selection in the first place. Good creators, like experts of any kind, may or may not have more ideas than other people have, but they have better ideas, ones that are more likely to be selectively retained. And the reason they are more likely to be selectively retained is that they were not produced in a blind fashion. This debate is by no means resolved, however, and is likely to continue.

If understanding creativity requires a multidisciplinary approach, then a unidisciplinary approach would view a part of the whole as the whole. At the same time we would have an incomplete explanation of the phenomenon we are seeking to explain. We believe that this has been the case for creativity. Recently, theorists have begun to develop confluence approaches to creativity, which we will now discuss.

☐ Confluence Approaches

Many recent works on creativity hypothesize that multiple components must converge for creativity to occur (Amabile, 1983; Csikszentmihalyi, 1988; Gardner, 1993; Gruber, 1989; Gruber & Wallace, 1999; Lubart, 1994; Mumford & Gustafson, 1988; Perkins, 1981; Simonton, 1988; Sternberg, 1985b; Sternberg & Lubart, 1991, 1995, 1996; Weisberg, 1993; Woodman & Schoenfeldt, 1989). Sternberg (1985b), for example, examined laypersons' and experts' conceptions of the creative person. People's implicit theories contain a combination of cognitive and personality elements, such as "connects ideas," "sees similarities and differences," "has flexibility," "has aesthetic taste," "is unorthodox," "is motivated," "is inquisitive," and "questions societal norms."

At the level of explicit theories, Amabile (1983, 1996; Collins & Amabile, 1999) describes creativity as the confluence of intrinsic motivation, domain-relevant knowledge and abilities, and creativity-relevant skills. The creativity-relevant skills include (a) a cognitive style that involves coping with complexities and breaking one's mental set during problem solving, (b) knowledge of heuristics for generating novel ideas, such as trying a counterintuitive approach, and (c) a work style characterized by concentrated effort, an ability to set aside problems, and high energy.

Gruber and his colleagues (1981, 1989; Gruber & Davis, 1988) have proposed a developmental *evolving-systems model* for understanding creativity. A person's knowledge, purpose, and affect grow over time, amplify deviations that an individual encounters, and lead to creative products. Developmental changes in the knowledge system have been documented in cases such as Charles Darwin's thoughts on evolution. Purpose refers to a set of interrelated goals, which also develop and guide an individual's behavior. Finally, the affect or mood system notes the influence of joy or frustration on the projects undertaken. Perhaps most interesting about Gruber's work is that it shows how the accumulation of long chains of evolutionary ideas can lead to revolutionary ideas. Darwin, for example, had many creative insights that were fairly minor forward incrementations, but when he combined them, he leaped to a reinitiation with respect to ideas of the time.

Csikszentmihalyi (1988, 1996) has taken a different "systems" approach and highlights the interaction of the individual, domain, and field. An individual draws upon information in a domain and transforms or extends it via cognitive processes, personality traits, and motivation. The field, consisting of people who control or influence a domain (e.g., art critics and gallery owners), evaluates and selects new ideas. The domain, a culturally defined symbol system such as alphabetic writing or mathematical notation or musical notation preserves and transmits creative products to other individuals and future generations. To some extent, the kind of creativity one shows will depend upon the extent to which one has internalized the values and reward systems of the paradigms governing the field. Those who want short-term rewards from the field are perhaps more likely to show evolutionary, paradigm-accepting forms of creativity. Those who go for the long term, however, may be willing to risk short-term disapprobation by the field and to propose more paradigm-rejecting ideas. The field acts as a largely conservative force upon the expansion of ideas within a domain, rewarding, for the most part, those ideas that accept current paradigms, and being, at best, skeptical of ideas that reject these paradigms.

Gardner (1993; see also Policastro & Gardner, 1999) has conducted case studies that suggest that the development of creative projects may stem from an anomaly within a system (e.g., tension between competing critics in a field) or moderate asynchronies between the individual, domain, and field (e.g., unusual individual talent for a domain). In particular, Gardner (1993) has analyzed the lives of seven individuals who made highly creative contributions in the twentieth century, with each specializing in one of the multiple intelligences (Gardner, 1983): Sigmund Freud (intrapersonal), Albert Einstein (logical-mathematical), Pablo Picasso (spatial), Igor Stravinsky (musical), T. S. Eliot (linguistic), Martha Graham (bodily-kinesthetic), and Mohandas Gandhi (interpersonal). Charles Darwin is an example of someone with extremely high naturalist intelligence. Gardner points out, however, that most of these individuals actually had strengths in more than one intelligence, and that they had notable weaknesses as well in others (e.g., Freud's weaknesses may have been in spatial and musical intelligences).

Although creativity can be understood in terms of uses of the multiple intelligences to generate new and even revolutionary ideas, Gardner's (1993) analysis goes well beyond the intellectual. For example, Gardner pointed out two major themes in the behavior of these creative giants. First, they tended to have a matrix of support at the time of their creative breakthroughs. Second, they tended to drive a "Faustian bargain" whereby they gave up many of the pleasures people typically enjoy in life in order to attain extraordinary success in their careers. It is not clear that these attributes are intrinsic to creativity per se; rather, they seem to be associated with those who have been driven to exploit their creative gifts in a way that leads them to attain eminence. Gardner's twentieth-century exemplars of creativity (such as Freud and Einstein) tended to be people who showed paradigm-breaking creativity (redirections and reinitiations), and people showing paradigm-accepting creativity might be less likely to show the traits Gardner isolated. For example, the greater social support received by people who show paradigm-accepting forms of creativity might lead such people to feel less or no need to drive a "Faustian bargain."

Gardner further followed Csikszentmihalyi (1988, 1996) in distinguishing between the importance of the domain (the body of knowledge about a particular subject area) and the field (the context in which this body of knowledge is studied and elaborated, including the persons working with the domain, such as critics, publishers, and other "gate-keepers"). Both are important to the development and, ultimately, the recognition of creativity.

A final confluence theory considered here is Sternberg and Lubart's (1991, 1995) *investment theory of creativity*. According to this theory, creative people are those who are willing and able to "buy low and sell high" in the realm of ideas (see also Rubenson & Runco, 1992, for use of concepts from economic theory). Buying low means pursuing ideas that are unknown or out of favor but that have growth potential. Often, when these ideas are first presented, they encounter resistance. The creative individual persists in the face of this resistance and eventually sells high, moving on to the next new or unpopular idea.

Preliminary research within the investment framework has yielded support for this model (Lubart & Sternberg, 1995). This research has used tasks such as (a) writing short stories with unusual titles (e.g., "The Octopus' Sneakers"), (b) drawing pictures with unusual themes (e.g., "the earth from an insect's point of view"), (c) devising creative advertisements for boring products (e.g., cufflinks), and (d) solving unusual scientific problems (e.g., how we could tell if someone had been on the moon within the past month). This research showed creative performance to be moderately domain specific, and to be predicted by a combination of certain resources, as described below.

According to the investment theory, creativity requires a confluence of six distinct but interrelated resources: intellectual abilities, knowledge, styles of thinking, personality, motivation, and environment.

Three intellectual abilities are particularly important (Sternberg, 1985a): (a) the synthetic ability to see problems in new ways and to escape the bounds of conventional thinking; (b) the analytic ability to recognize which of one's ideas are worth pursuing and which are not; and (c) the practical-contextual ability to know how to persuade (to sell) others on the value of one's ideas. The confluence of these three abilities is also important. Analytic ability used in the absence of the other two abilities results in powerful critical, but not creative, thinking. Synthetic ability in the absence of the other two abilities results in new ideas that are not subjected to the scrutiny required to make them work. And practical-contextual ability in the absence of the other two may result in the transmission of ideas not because the ideas are good, but, rather, because the ideas have been well and powerfully presented.

As regards knowledge, one must know enough about a field to move it forward. One cannot move the field if one does not know where it is. However, knowledge about a field can result in a closed and entrenched perspective, resulting in a person's inability to move beyond the way in which he or she has seen problems in the past (Frensch & Sternberg, 1989).

With regard to thinking styles, a legislative style is particularly important for creativity (Sternberg, 1988c, 1997), that is, a preference for thinking in new ways. This preference needs to be distinguished from the ability to think creatively: Someone may like to think along new lines, but not think well, or vice versa. To become a major creative thinker, it also helps if one is able to think globally as well as locally, distinguishing the forest from the trees and thereby recognizing which questions are important and which are not.

Numerous research investigations (summarized in Lubart, 1994, and Sternberg & Lubart, 1991, 1995) have supported the importance of certain personality attributes for creative functioning. These attributes include, but are not limited to, willingness to overcome obstacles, willingness to take sensible risks, willingness to tolerate ambiguity, and self-efficacy. In particular, buying low and selling high typically means defying the crowd, so that one has to be willing to stand up to conventions if one wants to think and act in creative ways.

Intrinsic, task-focused motivation is also essential to creativity. The research of Amabile (1983) and others has shown the importance of such motivation for creative work and has suggested that people rarely do truly creative work in an area unless they really love what they are doing and focus on the work rather than the potential rewards.

Finally, one needs an environment that supports and rewards creative ideas. One could have all of the internal resources needed in order to think creatively, but without some environmental support (such as a forum for proposing those ideas), the creativity that a person has within him or her might never be displayed.

Concerning the confluence of components, creativity is hypothesized to involve more than a simple sum of a person's level on each component. First, there may be thresholds for some components (e.g., knowledge) below which creativity is not possible regardless of the levels on other components. Second, partial compensation may occur in which a strength on one component (e.g., motivation) counteracts a weakness on another component (e.g., environment). Third, interactions may also occur between components, such as intelligence and motivation, in which high levels on both component could multiplicatively enhance creativity.

The investment theory of creativity provided part of the motivation for the formation of the propulsion model of creative contributions. The investment theory states that creative people "defy the crowd" by "buying low and selling high in the world of ideas." In other words, creative people are paradigm rejecting in their defiance. But as time passed after the initial proposal of the theory (Sternberg & Lubart, 1991), it became clear that not all creative people, and not all creative ideas, are paradigm defiant. So the theory seemed to apply to some kinds of creativity, but perhaps not to others. The propulsion model was, in part, an attempt to determine to what kinds of people and ideas, precisely, the investment theory applied.

In general, confluence theories of creativity offer the possibility of accounting for diverse aspects of creativity (Lubart, 1994). For example, analyses of scientific and artistic achievements suggest that the median creativity of work in a domain tends to fall toward the lower end of the distribution and the upper—high creativity—tail extends quite far. This pattern can be explained through the need for multiple components of creativity to cooccur in order for the highest levels of creativity to be achieved. As another example, the partial domain specificity of creativity that is often observed can be explained through the mixture of some relatively domain-specific components for creativity such as knowledge and other more domain-general components such as, perhaps, the personality trait of perseverance. Creativity, then, is largely something that people show in a particular domain.

CHAPTER

Conclusions

We have proposed a model of eight types of creative contributions that are linked by their adherence to a multidimensional spatial metaphor. What purposes might be served by this or any model of creative contributions?

First, these models capture the intuition that creative contributions differ not only in degree but also in kind. Some contributions seem to be largely incremental in nature, yet others seem to steer a field in a new direction. These other contributions redirect in different ways, however, some taking off from where the field is and others advancing from a different starting point. The propulsion model proposed here proposes within a unified framework a classification scheme for these and other different kinds of creative contributions.

Second, a model such as this one may be useful in properly judging the kinds as well as the levels of creativity that various individuals in a field show. An institution might decide that it values certain kinds of creative contributions more than others or that it requires members to make different kinds of creative contributions. The propulsion model can help characterize the work of various individuals and thus achieve a balance. It is important to remember, however, that the types of valuing we might do for these different kinds of creative contribution are subjective. There is no a priori scale that renders one kind of creative work "better" than other kinds.

Third, the model may be useful even in charting the progress of a field. For example, when a paradigm matures, such as cognitive-task analysis

119

has in the study of intelligence or attribution theory has in the study of social psychology, it becomes more and more difficult to make a distinctively new contribution to that paradigm. Often the questions seem to become smaller and smaller. When the rate of incrementations is slowing down or the amount of progress investigators are making in terms of forward movement in the multidimensional space seems to be shrinking, the investigators might want to consider the other contributions that can be made, as specified by the propulsion model.

Fourth, the model may help the members of a field recognize creative contributions they otherwise might overlook. It can also serve as a heuristic for the generation of a variety of creative ideas. Most creative contributions are probably incrementations, and these contributions are generally the easiest to recognize because they start where the field is and help move it further in its current direction. By evaluating creative work with the propulsion model in mind, an individual might recognize as creative, say, a redirection or even a reinitiation that he or she otherwise might have seen as departing too far from where the field is and should be.

Certain kinds of creative contributions may be, in practice, more highly creative than other kinds, but there can be no claim in principle that contributions of one kind are more creative than contributions of another kind (with the possible exception of replications typically being less creative). The reason is that any kind of contribution can vary in its novelty and quality vis-à-vis a given mission. Consider as an example a reinitiation versus a forward incrementation. A reinitiation is, on average, more defiant of existing paradigms than is a forward incrementation. But a reinitiation is not necessarily more creative than is a forward incrementation. The reinitiation may differ only trivially from existing paradigms or it may differ in a way that moves the field in a fruitless direction. The forward incrementation, on the other hand, may be one that has eluded all or almost all other investigators and thus is highly novel; moreover, it may be a contribution that adds just the step that makes a great difference to a field, such as the step that yields a vaccine against a serious illness. Thus, kinds of creative contributions do not immediately translate into levels of creative contributions. The relative levels of creativity of two contributions have to be determined on other grounds.

Nevertheless, individual investigators or institutions may have preferences for one kind of creative contribution over another. The management of one institution may feel threatened by redefinitions or reinitiations while the management of another institution welcomes them. One graduate advisor may encourage his or her students to strike out on their own in crowd-defying directions, whereas another graduate advisor prefers that students work only within existing paradigms or perhaps even only the advisor's own paradigm. Undoubtedly, graduate training plays an important role not only in socializing students with respect to doing worthwhile research but also with respect to the kinds of research that are considered to be worthwhile. As always, what is viewed as creative will depend upon the match between what an individual has to offer and what the context is willing to value. We also need to keep in mind that contributions are judged on the basis of many attributes, not just their creativity. A contribution that is creative may be valued or devalued in a society for any number of reasons, such as its "political correctness" or the gender, ethnic group, or status of its creator.

The propulsion model may help explain several creativity-related phenomena, although of course it does not provide a unique explanation.

First, the propulsion model may help account for the difficulty people might have in reconciling the notion that creativity tends to generate negative reactions with the notion that most people seem to believe that they support creativity (Sternberg & Lubart, 1995). The present model suggests that the positivity or negativity of reactions to a given contribution is likely to vary with the kind of creativity that is evinced in a given creative contribution. For example, the kind of paradigm-rejecting, crowd-defying creativity dealt with by the investment theory of creativity (Sternberg & Lubart, 1995) is probably largely of the last three kinds: redirection (5), reconstruction/redirection (6), and especially reinitiation (7). Paradigm-accepting creativity is more likely to generate a favorable response, at least initially. Forward incrementations, for example, are creative but occur within existing paradigms and hence are more likely to engender favorable reactions, whether from journal editors, grant reviewers, or critics of music and art. In the short run, artists, scientists, and others who provide forward incrementations may have the easiest time getting their work accepted; in the long run, however, their contributions may not be the longest lasting or the most important for the future of the field.

Second, the propulsion model helps psychologists better understand the relationship between creativity and leadership (see, e.g., Gardner, 1993, 1995). Leadership, like creativity, is propulsion. Hence, creativity always represents at least a weak attempt to lead. But in the case of replication, the attempt is rather trivial. In the case of redirection, reconstruction/redirection, or reinitiation, it may be quite dramatic. In each of these cases, the creative individual is trying to lead the field in a direction different from the one in which it is already moving. Even advance incrementation represents an impressive form of leadership, in that it attempts to lead a field rather far away from where it is in the multidimensional space, albeit in the same direction as the field already is going.

Examples of the application of the propulsion model to creative leadership can be inferred from an analysis of university presidents by Levine (1998). Levine provides examples of two failed presidents—Francis Wayland of Brown (president from 1827 to 1855) and Henry Tappan of the University of Michigan (1852 to 1863), both of whom failed because their ideas were ahead of their time. Their ideas would succeed in other institutions, but later. Both presidents exemplified forward advance incrementations in the attempts at creative leadership of their institutions. Robert Hutchins, president of the University of Chicago from 1929 to 1951, was removed from his presidency because his ideas were behind the times. Hutchins wished to set off in a new direction from a set of ideas that had become passé in the minds of his constituents. Hutchins illustrated reconstruction/redirection. Clark Kerr, president of the University of California, Berkeley, from 1959 to 1967, ultimately failed because he was the wrong person at the wrong time when Ronald Reagan became governor of California. In essence, Reagan moved the multidimensional space to a new point, one that left Kerr outside the realm that was viewed as acceptable. The mantle of creative leadership thus was taken on by a governor, who left the university president out of a job.

Third, the propulsion model helps address the question of whether programs based on artificial intelligence are creative (see discussions in Boden, 1990, 1999; Dreyfus, 1992). To the extent that computer programs *replicate* past discoveries, no matter how creative those discoveries were, they are nevertheless replications, which is creativity (1), although perhaps of a more modest type. Although computers may not be able to move a field forward or in a new direction, they may be creative in other ways. Our reading of the current literature is that these programs are certainly creative in the sense of replication and that they also probably have been creative in the sense of forward incrementations. It is not clear that they have shown the more crowd-defying forms of creativity (5–7: redirection, reconstruction/redirection, reinitiation).

Fourth, the propulsion model may be relevant to the long-standing issue (raised above) of the extent to which creativity is domain specific or domain general. We would speculate that the ability to perform reasonably successful forward incrementations may be largely domain general and may even be highly correlated with scores on tests of conventional (analytical) abilities. A forward incrementation seems to require, for the most part, extensive knowledge and an analysis of the trajectory of that field. The ability to acquire, understand, and analyze a knowledge base is largely what is measured by conventional standardized tests (Sternberg, 1997). But the ability to perform a reinitiation may be quite a bit more domain specific, requiring a sense or even feeling for a field that goes well beyond the kinds of more generalized analytical abilities measured by conventional tests. Indeed, people who engage in creativity of kinds 5 (redirection), 6 (reconstruction/redirection), and 7 (reinitiation) may be those who are less susceptible than others to the entrenchment that can accompany expertise (Frensch & Sternberg, 1989; Sternberg & Lubart, 1995).

The propulsion model certainly has weaknesses and ambiguities. First, it is new and has yet to be quantitatively tested. Such tests are planned, based on classifications of creative contributions and analyses of various measures of their impact. Second, contributions cannot be unequivocally classified into the different kinds. Bach, for example, was viewed in his time as, at best, making small forward incremental contributions or even as being a replicator. Today he is perceived by many as having helped to redefine Baroque music. Moreover, because we are always making judgments from our perspective, it is impossible to ensure "objective" judgments of the kind of creative contribution a particular work makes or has made. Third, the model proposed here is probably not exhaustive with respect to the kinds of creative contributions that can be made. There may well be others, and the ones proposed here almost certainly could be subdivided. Fourth, a given contribution may have elements of more than one kind of contribution. Finally, the spatial metaphor used as a basis for the theory obviously is an oversimplification. There is no one point in a multidimensional space that adequately can represent a field or a subfield, nor is all research in the field or subfield moving in a single direction.

Ultimately, it is unlikely that there is any one "right" model of kinds of creative contributions. Rather, models such as this one can help people expand their thinking about the kinds of creative contributions that can be made in a field. And to the extent this model accomplishes that goal, it is achieving what it should. Creative contributions differ not only in amounts but also in types, and the eight kinds represented here are ones that presumably occur in all fields at all times. We should be aware of them when they occur. We also may wish to steer our students and ourselves toward certain kinds of creative contributions, ideally the kinds that are most compatible with what these students or we, respectively, ideally wish to offer.

REFERENCES

Abelson, R. P., Aronson, E., McGuire, W. J., Newcomb, T. M., Rosenberg, M. J., & Tannenbaum, P. H. (Eds.). (1968). *Theories of cognitive consistency: A sourcebook.* Chicago: Rand McNally.

Adams, J. L. (1974). *Conceptual blockbusting: A guide to better ideas.* San Francisco: Freeman.

Adams, J. L. (1986). *The care and feeding of ideas: A guide to encouraging creativity.* Reading, MA: Addison-Wesley.

Albert, R. S., & Runco, M. A. (1999). A history of research on creativity. In R. J. Sternberg (Ed.), *Handbook of creativity* (pp. 16–31). New York: Cambridge University Press.

Alessandrini, G. (1984). *Forbidden Broadway.* New York: DRG Records.

Amabile, T. M. (1983). *The social psychology of creativity.* New York: Springer.

Amabile, T. M. (1996). *Creativity in context.* Boulder, CO: Westview.

Andrews, F. M. (1975). Social and psychological factors which influence the creative process. In I. A. Taylor & J. W. Getzels (Eds.), *Perspectives in creativity* (pp. 117–145). Chicago: Aldine.

Barron, F. (1963). *Creativity and psychological health.* Princeton, NJ: D. Van Nostrand.

Barron, F. (1968). *Creativity and personal freedom.* New York: Van Nostrand.

Barron, F. (1969). *Creative person and creative process.* New York: Holt, Rinehart & Winston.

Barron, F. (1988). Putting creativity to work. In R. J. Sternberg (Ed.), *The nature of creativity* (pp. 76–98). New York: Cambridge University Press.

Barron, F., & Harrington, D. M. (1981). Creativity, intelligence, and personality. *Annual Review of Psychology, 32,* 439–476.

Barton, F. (2001). *Forbidden Broadway* [On-line]. Available: http://www.fredbarton.com/forbidden_broadway.htm

Bateson, G. (1979). *Mind and nature.* London: Wildwood House.

Becker, E. (1973). *The denial of death.* New York: Macmillan.

Bem, D. J. (1967). Self-perception: An alternative interpretation of cognitive dissonance phenomena. *Psychological Review, 74,* 183–200.

Bem, D. J. (1996). Exotic becomes erotic: A developmental theory of sexual orientation. *Psychological Review, 103,* 320–335.

Binet, A., & Simon, T. (1916). *The development of intelligence in children.* Baltimore, MD: Williams & Wilkins. (Originally published in 1905)

Bloom, H. (1994). *The Western canon: The books and school of the ages.* New York: Harcourt Brace.

Boden, M. (1992). *The creative mind: Myths and mechanisms.* New York: Basic Books.

Boden, M. A. (1999). Computer models of creativity. In R. J. Sternberg (Ed.), *Handbook of creativity* (pp. 351–372). New York: Cambridge University Press.

Boller, Jr., P. F. (1984). *Presidential campaigns.* New York: Oxford University Press.

Boller, Jr., P. F. (1988). *Presidential wives.* New York: Oxford University Press.

Boller, Jr., P. F. (1991). *Congressional anecdotes*. New York: Oxford University Press.

Bosworth, P. (1995). *Diane Arbus: A biography*. New York: W. W. Norton.

Bowers, K. S., Regehr, G., Balthazard, C., & Parker, K. (1990). Intuition in the context of discovery. *Cognitive Psychology, 22*, 72–109.

Brand, C. (1996). *The g factor: General intelligence and its implications*. Chichester, England: Wiley.

Bransford, J. D., & Stein, B. (1984). *The IDEAL problem solver*. New York: Freeman.

Brooks, T., & Marsh, E. (1995). *The complete directory to prime time network and cable TV shows, 1946–present* (6th ed.) New York: Ballantine.

Bullivant, R. (1980). Fugue. In S. Sadie (Ed.), *The new Grove dictionary of music and musicians* (Vol. 7, pp. 9–21). London: Macmillan.

Burroughs, W. S. (1959). *Naked lunch*. New York: Grove Press.

Cage, J. (1961). *Silence*. Middletown, CT: Wesleyan University Press.

Campbell, D. T. (1960). Blind variation and selective retention in creative thought as in other knowledge processes. *Psychological Bulletin, 67*, 380–400.

Cardwell, D. (1994). *The Fontana history of science*. Fontana Press: London.

Carroll, J. B. (1982). The measurement of intelligence. In R. J. Sternberg (Ed.), *Handbook of human intelligence* (pp. 29–120). New York: Cambridge University Press.

Carroll, J. B. (1993). *Human cognitive abilities: A survey of factor-analytic studies*. New York: Cambridge University Press.

Ceci, S. J. (1996). *On intelligence: A bioecological treatise on intellectual development* (expanded ed.). Cambridge, MA: Harvard University Press.

Chomsky, N. (1957). *Syntactic structures*. The Hague, Netherlands: Mouton.

Christie, A. (1926). *The murder of Roger Ackroyd*. New York: Dodd, Mead.

Cialdini, R. (1984). *Influence: The psychology of persuasion*. New York: Quill Books.

Clark, R. W. (1985). *Works of man*. New York: Viking Press.

Clement, J. (1989). Learning via model construction and criticism: Protocol evidence on sources of creativity in science. In G. Glover, R. Ronning, & C. Reynolds (Eds.), *Handbook of creativity* (pp. 341–381). New York: Plenum.

Cohen, A. (1999, September 27). "The world according to . . . Pat Buchanan." *Time, 154*, pp. 46–47.

Cohen, I. B. (1985). *Revolution in science*. Cambridge, MA: Belknap/Harvard.

Collins, M. A., & Amabile, T. M. (1999). Motivation and creativity. In R. J. Sternberg (Ed.), *Handbook of creativity* (pp. 297–312). New York: Cambridge University Press.

Connolly, M. (2001). ABC Sports Online [On-line]. Available: http://www.abcsports.com/markmywords/dmiller.html

Cox, C. M. (1926). *The early mental traits of three hundred geniuses*. Stanford, CA: Stanford University Press.

Crissey, H. E. (1999). Baseball and World War II. In J. Thorn, P. Palmer, M. Gershman, & D. Pietrusza (Eds.), *Total baseball* (6th ed.). Kingston, NY: Total Sports Publishing.

Crutchfield, R. (1962). Conformity and creative thinking. In H. Gruber, G. Terrell, & M. Wertheimer (Eds.), *Contemporary approaches to creative thinking* (pp.120–140). New York: Atherton Press.

Csikszentmihalyi, M. (1988). Society, culture, and person: A systems view of creativity. In R. J. Sternberg (Ed.), *The nature of creativity* (pp. 325–339). New York: Cambridge University Press.

Csikszentmihalyi, M. (1996). *Creativity*. New York: HarperCollins.

Csikszentmihalyi, M. (1999). Implications of a systems perspective for the study of creativity. In R. J. Sternberg (Ed.), *Handbook of creativity* (pp. 313–335). New York: Cambridge University Press.

Csikszentmihalyi, M., & Rathunde, K. (1990). The psychology of wisdom: An evolutionary interpretation. In R. J. Sternberg (Ed.), *Wisdom: Its nature, origins, and development* (pp. 25–51). New York: Cambridge University Press.

Cziko, G. A. (1998). From blind to creative: In defense of Donald Campbell's selectionist theory of human creativity. *Journal of Creative Behavior, 32*, 192–209.

Dalek, M. (1995). The conservative 1960s: From the perspective of the 1990s, it's the big political story of the era. *The Atlantic Monthly, 276*(6), 130–135.

DeBono, E. (1971). *Lateral thinking for management.* New York: McGraw-Hill.

DeBono, E. (1985). *Six thinking hats.* Boston: Little, Brown.

DeBono, E. (1992). *Serious creativity: Using the power of lateral thinking to create new ideas.* New York: Harper Collins.

Derrida, J., & Attridge, D. (Eds.). (1992). *Acts of literature.* New York: Routledge.

Dorris, M., & Erdrich, L. (1992). *The crown of Columbus.* New York: Harper Collins.

Dreyfus, H. L. (1992). *What computers still can't do.* Cambridge, MA: MIT Press.

Drimmler, F. (1973). *Very special people.* New York: Amjon.

Duncker, K. (1945). On problem solving. *Psychological Monographs, 58*(5), 270.

Ellis, J. J. (1998). *American sphinx: The character of Thomas Jefferson.* New York: Vintage.

Eskin, B. (1998). *The book of political lists.* New York: Villard.

Eysenck, H. J. (1993). Creativity and personality: A theoretical perspective. *Psychological Inquiry, 4*, 147–178.

Fadiman, C. (Ed.). (1985). *The Little, Brown book of anecdotes.* Boston: Little, Brown, and Company.

Fastball. (1999). [On-line]. Available: http://www.fastball.com.

Fazio, R. H., Zanna, M. P., & Cooper, J. (1977). Dissonance and self perception: An integrative view of each theory's proper domain of application. *Journal of Experimental Social Psychology, 13*, 464–479.

Feist, G. J. (1999). The influence of personality on artistic and scientific creativity. In R. J. Sternberg (Ed.), *Handbook of creativity* (pp. 273–296). New York: Cambridge University Press.

Feldman, D. H. (1999). The development of creativity. In R. J. Sternberg (Ed.), *Handbook of creativity* (pp. 169–186). New York: Cambridge University Press.

Feldman, D. H., Csikszentmihalyi, M., & Gardner, H. (1994). *Changing the world: A framework for the study of creativity.* Westport, CT: Praeger.

Fernandez Retamar, R. (1989). *Caliban and other essays* (E. Baker, Trans.). Minneapolis: University of Minnesota Press.

Ferris, R. G. (1973). *Signers of the Declaration.* Washington, DC: United States Department of the Interior.

Festinger, L., & Carlsmith, J. M. (1959). Cognitive consequences of forced compliance. *Journal of Abnormal and Social Psychology, 58*, 203–210.

Findlay, C. S., & Lumsden, C. J. (1988). The creative mind: Toward an evolutionary theory of discovery and invention. *Journal of Social and Biological Structures, 11*, 3–55.

Finke, R. (1995). A. Creative insight and preinventive forms. In R. J. Sternberg & J. E. Davidson (Eds.), *The nature of insight* (pp. 255–280). Cambridge, MA: MIT Press.

Finke, R. A. (1990). *Creative imagery: Discoveries and inventions in visualization.* Hillsdale, NJ: Erlbaum.

Finke, R. A., Ward, T. B., & Smith, S. M. (1992). *Creative cognition: Theory, research, and applications.* Cambridge, MA: MIT Press.

Flatow, I. (1992). *They all laughed . . .* Harper Collins: New York.

Flescher, I. (1963). Anxiety and achievement of intellectually gifted and creatively gifted children. *Journal of Psychology, 56*, 251–268.

Frank, A. M. (1952). *The diary of Anne Frank* (B. M. Mooyaart-Doubleday, Trans.). New York: Doubleday.

Frank, M., Ziebarth, M., & Field, C. (1982). *The life and times of Rosie the Riveter: The story of three million working women during World War II.* Emeryville, CA: Clarity Educational Productions.

Frensch, P. A., & Sternberg, R. J. (1989). Expertise and intelligent thinking: When is it worse to know better? In R. J. Sternberg (Ed.), *Advances in the psychology of human intelligence* (Vol. 5, pp. 157–188). Hillsdale, NJ: Erlbaum.

Freud, S. (1959). The relation of the poet to day-dreaming. In E. Jones (Ed.), *Collected papers* (Vol. 4, pp. 173–183). London: Hogarth. (Original work published in 1908)

Freud, S. (1964). *Leonardo da Vinci and a memory of his childhood.* New York: Norton. (Original work published in 1910)

Galton, F. (1869). *Heredity genius: An inquiry into its laws and consequences.* London: Macmillan.

Galton, F. (1883). *Inquiry into human faculty and its development.* London: Macmillan.

Gardner, H. (1983). *Frames of mind: The theory of multiple intelligences.* New York: Basic.

Gardner, H. (1993). *Creating minds.* New York: Basic Books.

Gardner, H. (1994). The creator's patterns. In D. H. Feldman, M. Csikszentmihalyi, & H. Gardner (Eds.), *Changing the world: A framework for the study of creativity* (pp. 69–84). Westport, CT: Praeger.

Gardner, H. (1995). *Leading minds.* New York: Basic Books.

Getzels, J. W., & Csikszentmihalyi, M. (1976). *The creative vision: A longitudinal study of problem finding in art.* New York: Wiley.

Getzels, J. W., & Jackson, P. W. (1962). *Creativity and intelligence: Explorations with gifted students.* New York: John Wiley & Sons.

Ghiselin, B. (Ed.). (1985). *The creative process: A symposium.* Berkeley: University of California Press.

Gleitman, H. (1986). *Psychology* (2nd ed.). New York: W.W. Norton & Co.

Golann, S. E. (1962). The creativity motive. *Journal of Personality, 30,* 588–600.

Goldwater, B. (1960). *The conscience of a conservative.* Shepherdsville, KY: Victor.

Gordon, J. S. (1999). *The great game: The emergence of Wall Street as a world power, 1653–2000.* New York: Scribner's.

Gordon, W. J. J. (1961). *Synectics: The development of creative capacity.* New York: Harper & Row.

Gough, H. G. (1979). A creativity scale for the Adjective Check List. *Journal of Personality and Social Psychology, 37,* 1398–1405.

Gough, H. G., & Woodworth, D. G. (1960). Stylistic variations among professional research scientists. *Journal of Psychology, 49,* 87–98.

Gould, S. J. (1981). *The mismeasure of man.* New York: Norton.

Graver, L. (1995). *An obsession with Anne Frank.* Berkeley: University of California Press.

Greenstein, G. (1998). *Portraits of discovery: Profiles in scientific genius.* New York: John Wiley & Sons.

Gruber, H. (1981). *Darwin on man: A psychological study of scientific creativity* (2nd ed.). Chicago: University of Chicago Press.

Gruber, H. E. (1989). The evolving systems approach to creative work. In D. B. Wallace & H. E. Gruber (Eds.), *Creative people at work: Twelve cognitive case studies* (pp. 3–24). New York: Oxford University Press.

Gruber, H. E., & Davis, S. N. (1988). Inching our way up Mount Olympus: The evolving-systems approach to creative thinking. In R. J. Sternberg (Ed.), *The nature of creativity* (pp. 243–270). New York: Cambridge University Press.

Gruber, H. E., & Wallace, D. B. (1999). The case study method and evolving systems approach for understanding unique creative people at work. In R. J. Sternberg (Ed.), *Handbook of creativity* (pp. 93–115). New York: Cambridge University Press.

Guilford, J. P. (1950). Creativity. *American Psychologist, 5,* 444–454.

Guilford, J. P. (1967). *The nature of human intelligence.* New York: McGraw-Hill.

Guilford, J. P. (1968). *Intelligence, creativity, and their educational implications.* San Diego, CA: Knapp.

Guilford, J. P. (1975). Creativity: A quarter century of progress. In I. A. Taylor & J. W. Getzels (Eds.), *Perspectives in creativity* (pp. 37–59). Chicago: Aldine.

Haley, J. (1969). *The power tactics of Jesus Christ, and other essays.* New York: Grossman.

Hamm, C. (1980). John Cage. In *The new Grove dictionary of music and musicians* (Vol. 3, pp. 597–603). London: Macmillan.

Harris, R. (1992). *Fatherland.* New York: Random House.

Harris, T. (1988). *Silence of the lambs.* New York: St. Martin's Press.

Hartt, F. (1993). *Art: A history of painting, sculpture, architecture* (4th ed). Englewood Cliffs, NJ: Prentice-Hall.

Hay, P. (1988). *The book of business anecdotes.* New York: Facts on File Publications.

Hayes, J. R. (1989). Cognitive processes in creativity. In J. A. Glover, R. R. Ronning, & C. R. Reynolds (Eds.), *Handbook of creativity* (pp. 135–145). New York: Plenum.

Hennessey, B. A., & Amabile, T. M. (1988). The conditions of creativity. In R. J. Sternberg (Ed.), *The nature of creativity* (pp. 11–38). New York: Cambridge University Press.

Herr, E. L., Moore, G. D., & Hasen, J. S. (1965). Creativity, intelligence, and values: A study of relationships. *Exceptional Children, 32,* 114–115.

Herrnstein, R. J., & Murray, C. (1994). *The bell curve.* New York: Free Press.

History of the organization of work. (2000). In Encyclopaedia Britannica. [On-line]. Available: http://www.britannica.com/bcom/eb/article/printable/1/0.5722.115711.00.html

Hodge, M. J. S. (1990). Origins and species before and after Darwin. In R. C. Olby, G. N. Canton, J. R. R. Christie, & M. J. S. Hodge (Eds.), *Companion to the history of modern science* (pp. 374–395). New York: Routledge.

Honey, M. (1984). *Creating Rosie the Riveter: Class, gender, and propaganda during World War II.* Amherst: University of Massachusetts Press.

Horn, J. L. (1994). Theory of fluid and crystallized intelligence. In R. J. Sternberg (Ed.), *The encyclopedia of human intelligence* (Vol. 1, pp. 443–451). New York: Macmillan.

Hunt, E., Frost, N., & Lunneborg, C. (1973). Individual differences in cognition: A new approach to intelligence. In G. Bower (Ed.), *The psychology of learning and motivation* (Vol. 7, pp. 87–122). New York: Academic Press.

Hunt, E. B., Lunneborg, C., & Lewis, J. (1975). What does it mean to be high verbal? *Cognitive Psychology, 7,* 194–227.

James, P., & Thorpe, N. (1994). *Ancient inventions.* Ballantine Books: New York.

Jay, R. (1986). *Learned pigs and fireproof women.* New York: Warner.

Jensen, A. R. (1982). Reaction time and psychometric g. In H. J. Eysenck (Ed.), *A model for intelligence* (pp. 93–132). Heidelberg, Germany: Springer-Verlag.

Jensen, A. R. (1998). *The g factor: The science of mental ability.* Westport, CT: Praeger/Greenwood.

Johnson, G. (2000, July 12). 100 years and miles to go. *Los Angeles Times,* p. G-1.

Johnson-Laird, P. N. (1988). *The computer and the mind: An introduction to cognitive science.* Cambridge, MA: Harvard University Press.

Kamin, L. (1974). *The science and politics of IQ.* Hillsdale, NJ: Erlbaum.

Kaplan, C. A., & Simon, H. A. (1990). In search of insight. *Cognitive Psychology, 22,* 374–419.

Kemp, I. (1980). Paul Hindemith. In *The new Grove dictionary of music and musicians* (Vol. 8, pp. 573–587). London: Macmillan.

Kipling, R. (1985). Working-tools. In B. Ghiselin (Ed.), *The creative process: A symposium* (pp. 161–163). Berkeley: University of California Press. (Original work published 1937)

Kirchner, P. (1996). *Oops! A stupefying survey of goofs, blunders & blotches, great & small.* Los Angeles: General Publishing Group.

Kirton, M. J., Bailey, A., & Glendinning, W. (1991). Adaptors and innovators: Preferences for educational procedures. *Journal of Psychology, 125,* 445–455.

Koestler, A. (1964). *The act of creation*. New York: Macmillan.

Kris, E. (1952). *Psychoanalytic exploration in art*. New York: International Universities Press.

Kubie, L. S. (1958). *The neurotic distortion of the creative process*. Lawrence: University of Kansas Press.

Kuhn, T. S. (1970). *The structure of scientific revolutions* (2nd ed.). Chicago: University of Chicago Press.

Kuhn, M., Long, C., & Quinn, L. (1991). *No stone unturned: The life and times of Maggie Kuhn*. New York: Ballantine.

Langley, P., Simon, H. A., Bradshaw, G. L., & Zytkow, J. M. (1987). *Scientific discovery: Computational explorations of the creative process*. Cambridge, MA: MIT Press.

Levine, A. (1998). Succeeding as a leader; failing as a president. *Change*, January/February, 43–45.

Lewontin, R. (1982). *Human diversity*. New York: Freeman.

Light, A. (Ed.). (1999). *Vibe history of Hip Hop*. New York: Three Rivers.

Lipstadt, D. E. (1993). *Denying the Holocaust: The growing assault on truth and memory*. New York: Free Press.

Lubart, T. I. (1990). Creativity and cross-cultural variation. *International Journal of Psychology, 25*, 39–59.

Lubart, T. I. (1994). Creativity. In R. J. Sternberg (Ed.), *Thinking and problem solving* (pp. 290–332). San Diego, CA: Academic Press.

Lubart, T. I., & Sternberg, R. J. (1995). An investment approach to creativity: Theory and data. In S. M. Smith, T. B. Ward, & R. A. Finke (Eds.), *The creative cognition approach* (pp. 269–302). Cambridge, MA: MIT Press.

Machlis, J. (1979). *Introduction to contemporary music*. (2nd ed.). New York: Norton.

MacKinnon, D. W. (1965). Personality and the realization of creative potential. *American Psychologist, 20*, 273–281.

Maduro, R. (1976). Artistic creativity in a Brahmin painter community. Research monograph 14, Berkeley: Center for South and Southeast Asia Studies, University of California.

Martindale, C. (1990). *The clockwork muse: The predictability of artistic change*. New York: Basic Books.

Martindale, C. (1999). Biological bases of creativity. In R. J. Sternberg (Ed.), *Handbook of creativity* (pp. 137–152). New York: Cambridge University Press.

Maslow, A. (1967). The creative attitude. In R. L. Mooney & T. A. Rasik (Eds.), *Explorations in creativity* (pp. 43–57). New York: Harper & Row.

Maslow, A. (1968). *Toward a psychology of being*. New York: Van Nostrand.

Maxwell, J. C. (1873/1991). *Treatise on electricity and magnetism*. Mineola, NY: Dover Publications.

McClelland, D. C., Atkinson, J. W., Clark, R. A., & Lowell, E. L. (1953). *The achievement motive*. New York: Appleton-Century-Crofts, Inc.

McNemar, Q. (1964). Lost: Our intelligence? Why? *American Psychologist, 19*, 871–882.

Meadows, J. (Ed.). (1987). *The history of scientific discovery*. Phaidon: Oxford.

Mednick, M. T., & Andrews, F. M. (1967). Creative thinking and level of intelligence. *Journal of Creative Behavior, 1*, 428–431.

Mednick, S. A. (1962). The associative basis of the creative process. *Psychological Review, 69*, 220–232.

Michael, W. B., & Wright, C. R. (1989). Psychometric issues in the assessment of creativity. In J. A. Glover, R. R. Ronning, & C. R. Reynolds (Eds.), *Handbook of creativity* (pp. 33–52). New York: Plenum.

Microsoft. (2000). *Acupuncture*. In Microsoft® Encarta® Online Encyclopedia. [On-line]. Available: http://encarta.msn.com.

Miyagawa, S. (2000). *The Japanese Language*. [On-line]. Available: http://www-japan.mit.edu/articles/ JapaneseLanguage.html

Mumford, M. D., & Gustafson, S. B. (1988). Creativity syndrome: Integration, application, and innovation. *Psychological Bulletin, 103*, 27–43.

Noy, P. (1969). A revision of the psychoanalytic theory of the primary process. *International Journal of Psychoanalysis, 50*, 155–178.

O'Brien, T. (1990). *The things they carried.* Boston: Houghton Mifflin.

Ochse, R. (1990). *Before the gates of excellence.* New York: Cambridge University Press.

Osborn, A. F. (1953). *Applied imagination* (rev. ed.). New York: Charles Scribner's Sons.

Panati, C. (1989). *Panati's extraordinary endings of practically everything and everybody.* New York: Harper & Row.

Panati, C. (1991). *Panati's parade of fads, follies, and manias.* New York: HarperPerennial.

Panati, C. (1998). *Sexy origins and intimate things.* New York: Penguin.

Parker, P., & Kermode, F. (Eds.). (1996). *A reader's guide to twentieth-century writers.* New York: Oxford University Press.

Perkins, D. N. (1981). *The mind's best work.* Cambridge, MA: Harvard University Press.

Perkins, D. N. (1995). Insight in minds and genes. In R. J. Sternberg & J. E. Davidson (Eds.), *The nature of insight* (pp. 495–534). Cambridge, MA: MIT Press.

Perkins, D. N. (1998). In the country of the blind: An appreciation of Donald Campbell's vision of creative thought. *Journal of Creative Behavior, 32*(3), 177–191.

Plucker, J. A., & Renzulli, J. S. (1999). Psychometric approaches to the study of human creativity. In R. J. Sternberg (Ed.), *Handbook of creativity* (pp. 35–61). New York: Cambridge University Press.

Policastro, E., & Gardner, H. (1999). From case studies to robust generalizations: An approach to the study of creativity. In R. J. Sternberg (Ed.), *Handbook of creativity* (pp. 213–225). New York: Cambridge University Press.

Raftery, B. M. (2000, June 9). Movies of the weak. *Entertainment Weekly, 544*, 59.

Rashke, R. (1987). *Escape from Sobibor.* New York: Avon.

Renzulli, J. S. (1986). The three-ring conception of giftedness: a developmental model for creative productivity. In R. J. Sternberg & J. E. Davidson (Eds.), *Conceptions of giftedness* (pp. 53–92). New York: Cambridge University Press.

Rhys, J. (1966). *Wide Sargasso Sea.* London: Deutsch.

Roe, A. (1952). *The making of a scientist.* New York: Dodd, Mead.

Roe, A. (1972). Patterns of productivity of scientists. *Science, 176*, 940–941.

Rogers, C. R. (1954). Toward a theory of creativity. *ETC: A Review of General Semantics, 11*, 249–260.

Rosch, E. (1978). Principles of categorization. In E. Rosch & B. B. Lloyd (Eds.), *Cognition and categorization* (pp. 27–48). Hillsdale, NJ: Erlbaum.

Rothenberg, A. (1979). *The emerging goddess.* Chicago: University of Chicago Press.

Rothenberg, A., & Hausman, C. R. (Eds.). (1976). *The creativity question.* Durham, NC: Duke University Press.

Royer, F. L. (1971). Information processing of visual figures in the digit symbol substitution task. *Journal of Experimental Psychology, 87*, 335–342.

Rubenson, D. L., & Runco, M. A. (1992). The psychoeconomic approach to creativity. *New Ideas in Psychology, 10*, 131–147.

Rubenstein, G. (2000). Gutenberg and the Historical Movement in Western Europe. [On-line]. Available: http://www.digitalcentury.com/encyclo/update/print.html

Safire, W. (1996). Standing history still: A prolegomenon. In P. Galassi & S. Kismaric (Eds.), *Pictures of the Times: A century of photography from the New York Times.* New York: The Museum of Modern Art.

Scarborough, K. (2001). *Futurism: Manifestos and other resources* [On-line]. Available: http://www.unknown.nu/futurism

Schleuning, P. (1993). *Johann Sebastian Bach's "Kunst der Fuge."* New York: Barenreiter-Verlag.

Schwartz, C. (1973). *Gershwin, his life and music.* New York: Da Capo.

Schwartz, C. (1980). George Gershwin. In *The new Grove dictionary of music and musicians* (Vol. 7, pp. 302–304). London: Macmillan.

Siegler, R. S. (1992). The other Alfred Binet. *Developmental Psychology, 28,* 179–190.

Silver, H. R. (1981). Calculating risks: The socioeconomic foundations of aesthetic innovation in an Ashanti carving community. *Ethnology, 20*(2), 101–114.

Silvers, R. (1997). *Photomosaics.* New York: Henry Holt.

Simonton, D. K. (1976). Biographical determinants of achieved eminence: A multivariate approach to the Cox data. *Journal of Personality and Social Psychology, 33,* 218–226.

Simonton, D. K. (1984). *Genius, creativity, and leadership.* Cambridge, MA: Harvard University Press.

Simonton, D. K. (1988). Age and outstanding achievement: What do we know after a century of research? *Psychological Bulletin, 104,* 251–267.

Simonton, D. K. (1994). *Greatness: Who makes history and why?* New York: Guilford.

Simonton, D. K. (1995). Foresight in insight: A Darwinian answer. In R. J. Sternberg & J. E. Davidson (Eds.), *The nature of insight* (pp. 495–534). Cambridge, MA: MIT Press.

Simonton, D. K. (1996). Creative expertise: A life-span developmental perspective. In K. A. Ericsson (Ed.), *The road to excellence* (pp. 227–253). Mahwah, NJ: Lawrence Erlbaum Associates.

Simonton, D. K. (1997). Creative productivity: A predictive and explanatory model of career trajectories and landmarks. *Psychological Review, 104,* 66–89.

Simonton, D. K. (1998). Donald Campbell's model of the creative process: Creativity as blind variation and selective retention. *Journal of Creative Behavior, 32,* 153–158.

Simonton, D. K. (1999). Creativity from a historiometric perspective. In R. J. Sternberg (Ed.), *Handbook of creativity* (pp. 116–133). New York: Cambridge University Press.

Singer, J. A. (2000). *Acupuncture, a brief introduction.* [On-line]. Available: http://216.92.231.12/Acup/Acupuncture.htm

Skinner, B. F. (1972). A behavioral model of creation. In B. F. Skinner (Ed.), *Cumulative record: A selection of papers* (pp. 345, 350–355). Englewood Cliffs, NJ: Prentice-Hall.

Smith, S. M., Ward, T. B., & Finke, R. A. (Eds.). (1995). *The creative cognition approach.* Cambridge, MA: MIT Press.

Spearman, C. E. (1904). "General intelligence" objectively determined and measured. *American Journal of Psychology, 15,* 201–293.

Spearman, C. (1927). *The abilities of man.* London: Macmillan.

Stein, L. (Ed.). (1975). *Style and idea: Selected writings of Arnold Schoenberg* (L. Black, Trans.). New York: St. Martin's Press.

Stern, S. L., & Schoenhaus, T. (1990*). Toyland: The high-stakes game of the toy industry.* New York: Contemporary.

Sternberg, R. J. (1977). *Intelligence, information processing, and analogical reasoning: The componential analysis of human abilities.* Hillsdale, NJ: Erlbaum.

Sternberg, R. J. (1983). Components of human intelligence. *Cognition, 15,* 1–48.

Sternberg, R. J. (1985a). *Beyond IQ: A triarchic theory of human intelligence.* New York: Cambridge University Press.

Sternberg, R. J. (1985b). Implicit theories of intelligence, creativity, and wisdom. *Journal of Personality and Social Psychology, 49*(3), 607–627.

Sternberg, R. J. (Ed.). (1988a). *The nature of creativity: Contemporary psychological perspectives.* New York: Cambridge University Press.

Sternberg, R. J. (1988b). Survival of the fittest in theories of creativity. *Journal of Social and Biological Structures, 11,* 154–155.

Sternberg, R. J. (1988c). Mental self-government: A theory of intellectual styles and their development. *Human Development, 31*(4), 197–224.

Sternberg, R. J. (1995). For whom the bell curve tolls: A review of *The Bell Curve*. *Psychological Science, 6,* 257–261.

Sternberg. R. J. (1996). IQ counts, but what really counts is successful intelligence. *NASSP Bulletin, 80,* 18–23.

Sternberg, R. J. (1997). *Successful intelligence.* New York: Plume.

Sternberg, R. J. (1998). Cognitive mechanisms in human creativity: Is variation blind or sighted? *Journal of Creative Behavior, 32,* 159–176.

Sternberg, R. J. (1999a). A dialectical basis for understanding the study of cognition. In R. J. Sternberg (Ed.), *The nature of cognition* (pp. 51–78). Cambridge, MA: MIT Press.

Sternberg, R. J. (Ed.). (1999b). *Handbook of creativity.* New York: Cambridge University Press.

Sternberg, R. J. (1999c). A propulsion model of types of creative contributions. *Review of General Psychology, 3,* 83–100.

Sternberg, R. J., & Davidson, J. E. (Eds.). (1994). *The nature of insight.* Cambridge, MA: MIT Press.

Sternberg, R. J., Kaufman, J. C., & Pretz, J. E. (2001). The propulsion model of creative contributions applied to the arts and letters. *Journal of Creative Behavior, 35,* 75–101.

Sternberg, R. J., & Lubart, T. I. (1991). An investment theory of creativity and its development. *Human Development, 34,* 1–31.

Sternberg, R. J., & Lubart, T. I. (1995). *Defying the crowd: Cultivating creativity in a culture of conformity.* New York: Free Press.

Sternberg, R. J., & Lubart, T. I. (1996). Investing in creativity. *American Psychologist, 51,* 677–688.

Sternberg, R. J., & Lubart, T. I. (1999). The concept of creativity: Prospects and paradigms. In R. J. Sternberg (Ed.), *Handbook of creativity* (pp. 3–15). New York: Cambridge University Press.

Sternberg, R. J., & O'Hara, L. (1999) Creativity and intelligence. In R. J. Sternberg (Ed.), *Handbook of creativity* (pp. 251–272). New York: Cambridge University Press.

Sternberg, R. J., Tourangeau, R., & Nigro, G. (1979). Metaphor, induction, and social policy: The convergence of macroscopic and microscopic views. In A. Ortony (Ed.), *Metaphor and thought* (pp. 325–353). New York: Cambridge University Press.

Suler, J. R. (1980). Primary process thinking and creativity. *Psychological Bulletin, 88,* 555–578.

Suskin, S. (1990). *Opening night on Broadway.* New York: Schirmer Books.

Suskin, S. (1997). *More opening nights on Broadway.* New York: Schirmer Books.

Thagard, P. (1992). *Conceptual revolutions.* Princeton, NJ: Princeton University Press.

Thomson, G. H. (1939). *The factorial analysis of human ability.* London: University of London Press.

Thurstone, L. L. (1938). *Primary mental abilities.* Chicago, IL: University of Chicago Press.

Tolman, E. C. (1932). *Purposive behavior in animals and men.* New York: Appleton-Century-Crofts.

Torrance, E. P. (1962). *Guiding creative talent.* Englewood Cliffs, NJ: Prentice-Hall.

Torrance, E. P. (1974). *Torrance tests of creative thinking.* Lexington, MA: Personnel Press.

Tourangeau, R., & Sternberg, R. J. (1981). Aptness in metaphor. *Cognitive Psychology, 13,* 27–55.

Tourangeau, R., & Sternberg, R. J. (1982). Understanding and appreciating metaphors. *Cognition, 11,* 203–244.

Turing, A. (1936–7). On computable numbers, with an application to the Entscheidungs problem. *Proceedings at the London Mathematical Society, 2*(42), 230–265.

Vernon, P. A., & Mori, M. (1992). Intelligence, reaction times, and peripheral nerve conduction velocity. *Intelligence, 8,* 273–288.

Vernon, P. E. (Ed.). (1970). *Creativity: Selected readings* (pp. 126–136). Baltimore, MD: Penguin Books.

Vogler, D. (1998). An overview of the history of the Japanese language. [On-line]. Available: http://humanities.byu.edu/classes/ling450ch/reports/japanese.htm

von Oech, R. (1983). *A whack on the side of the head.* New York: Warner.

von Oech, R. (1986). *A kick in the seat of the pants.* New York: Harper & Row.

Vonnegut, K. (1969). *Slaughterhouse five.* New York: Delacorte.

Wallace, J. (Ed.) (1995). *The baseball anthology: 125 years of stories, poems, articles, photographs, drawings, interviews, cartoons, and other memorabilia.* New York: Abradale.

Wallach, M. & Kogan, N. (1965). *Modes of thinking in young children.* New York: Holt, Rinehart, & Winston.

Ward, T. B. (1994). Structured imagination: The role of category structure in exemplar generation. *Cognitive Psychology, 27,* 1–40.

Ward, T. B., Smith, S. M., & Finke, R. A. (1999). Creative cognition. In R. J. Sternberg (Ed.), *Handbook of creativity* (pp. 189–212). New York: Cambridge University Press.

Wechsler, D. (1939). *The measurement of adult intelligence.* Baltimore, MD: Williams & Wilkins.

Wehner, L., Csikszentmihalyi, M., & Magyari-Beck, I. (1991). Current approaches used in studying creativity: An exploratory investigation. *Creativity Research Journal, 4*(3), 261–271.

Weisberg, R. W. (1986). *Creativity, genius and other myths.* New York: Freeman.

Weisberg, R. W. (1988). Problem solving and creativity. In R. J. Sternberg (Ed.), *The nature of creativity* (pp. 148–176). New York: Cambridge University Press.

Weisberg, R. W. (1993). *Creativity: Beyond the myth of genius.* New York: Freeman.

Weisberg, R. W. (1999). Creativity and knowledge: A challenge to theories. In R. J. Sternberg (Ed.), *Handbook of creativity* (pp. 226–250). New York: Cambridge University Press.

Weisberg, R. W. & Alba, J. W. (1981). An examination of the alleged role of "fixation" in the solution of several "insight" problems. *Journal of Experimental Psychology: General, 110,* 169–192.

Werner, H., & Kaplan, B. (1963). *Symbol formation.* Hillsdale, NJ: Erlbaum.

Wickett, J. C., & Vernon, P. A. (1994). Peripheral nerve conduction velocity, reaction time, and intelligence: An attempt to replicate Vernon and Mori. *Intelligence, 18,* 127–132.

Wiesenthal, S. (1967). *The murderers among us.* New York: McGraw Hill.

Williams, T. I. (1987). *The history of invention.* New York: Facts on File.

Woodman, R. W., & Schoenfeldt, L. F. (1989). Individual differences in creativity: An interactionist perspective. In J. A. Glover, R. R. Ronning, & C. R. Reynolds (Eds.), *Handbook of creativity.* New York: Plenum.

Yamamoto, K. (1964). Creativity and sociometric choice among adolescents. *Journal of Social Psychology, 64,* 249–261.

Yarwood, D. (1983). *Five hundred years of technology in the home.* London: B.T. Batsford.

Zadan, C. (1989). *Sondheim & Co.* (2nd ed.) New York: Harper and Row.

Zahoor, A. (1999). Sequoyah and Cherokee syllabary. [On-line]. Available: http://salam.muslimsonline.com/~azahoor/sequoyah1.htm

Zehme, B. (1999). *Lost in the funhouse: The life and mind of Andy Kaufman.* New York: Delacorte.

Zmuda, B., & Hansen, M. S. (1999). *Andy Kaufman revealed!: Best friend tells all.* New York: Little, Brown, and Company.

AUTHOR INDEX

SUBJECT INDEX

WITHDRAWN